Ref. TP–1094

TEXTILEPEDIA

THE COMPLETE FABRIC GUIDE

PLEASE READ INTRODUCTION
BEFORE USING
📖 ⊠   KEEP AWAY FROM FIRE   ⊠ ⊠

FASHIONARY

ISBN 978-988-77110-9-4
SN TPV152308PBCB

Designed and published in Hong Kong
by Fashionary International Ltd
Printed in China

Textilepedia is an ongoing project. If you have any
feedback, please don't hesitate to send it to
feedback@fashionary.org

🄵 @ fashionary
🄾 @ fashionary
🄿 @ fashionary

Fashionary Team 2023

THE
COMPLETE

FABRIC
GUIDE

PREFACE

by Fashionary Team

Fabric is a core part of the fashion industry. While the ideas behind clothing designs are vital to the creation of garments, fabrics are the foundation that supports these creative ideas.

Designers tend to focus on aesthetics; however, they should consider the materials as well. From fiber to fabric, every part is crucial to the outcome of a piece of clothing. A professional designer must have strong fabric knowledge to achieve better results, no matter whether they are designing for function or form.

Our goal with Textilepedia is to offer a practical, easy-to-read guide that equips designers with essential fabric knowledge. We have collaborated with industry experts to decipher the most crucial information about materials, and have presented it concisely with the aid of illustrations, comparisons, and relatable stories.

We hope that by reading Textilepedia, you will feel inspired and educated. This resource will also be useful for creating a design or collection, in addition to being a handy tool throughout your fashion career.

CONTENTS

CONTENTS

Q&A

FABRICS

01

How can the quality of fabric be defined?

While there is no definitive answer, the quality of fabric can be defined by examining various elements. Fabrics can be compared across different fabrications, paying particular attention to yarn count (measuring yarn quality) and thread count (measuring fabric density). A fabric works best when the functions fit the needs of the end product.

02

What affects the price of fabric?

Everything from fibers and finishings to the manufacturers and shops that sell the fabrics.

03

How and why do you weight fabric?

Fabrics can be weighed by grams per square meter (GSM) or ounce per square yard (OZ).

GSM	Grams per 1 square meter
OZ	Ounce per square yard

Although the weight of fabric is not necessarily equal to quality and thickness, it is a key factor to consider when choosing between similar fabrics. Fabric weight affects the final application of the fabric. Usually, lightweight fabrics are used for summer items or underwear, and heavyweight fabrics are used for upholstery or workwear.

04

Why do fabrics have different widths?

Fabric width is associated with the type of application, and also depends on the manufacturer. Commonly, the width of fabric is between 45 and 60 inches, but this can range from 35 to 108 inches. Interfacing comes in a narrow width of only 20 inches.

COMMON FABRIC WIDTH	COMMON APPLICATION
36"	Vintage fabric
45"	Quilting cotton and apparel fabric
54"	Upholstery and home decorating
60"	Non-standard apparel fabric

05

Why is the content of labels not always in the same format?

Clothing labels often include information about fiber content, country of origin, manufacturer identity, and care instructions. Information on these labels is usually bound by laws and regulations, and mandatory information is required in certain countries. As such, labels from various countries can appear quite different.

06 Is there an easy way to identify fabric content?

The easiest way to identify fabric is by touch; however, this is not always accurate. A heating and burning test is a simple, non-technical, but directional method used to identify groups of textile fibers. This technique defines whether the fibers are natural or synthetic. Other tests include microscopic identification and chemical tests.

07 Do textiles have an expiry date?

While textiles do not technically have an expiry date, their color and texture can change after wearing and washing. The condition of fabric usually depends on the handling and washing process.

08 Which fabrics do not cause allergies?

Breathable fabrics made from natural fibers, such as cotton and silk, are less likely to cause allergies.

09 What are sustainable textiles?

Sustainable textiles are those produced in ethically responsible ways. They can briefly be defined by three primary components: environmental, economic, and social sustainability, where environmental sustainability is generally more obvious, and features more often.

FIBERS

10 How many types of fibers are available in the market?

Fibers are generally divided into three types: natural, regenerated, and synthetic. They all have different characteristics and suit different applications.

11 Is natural or synthetic fiber a better option?

Neither better nor worse – it depends on what you are looking for. No fiber is perfect and there are pros and cons to each.

12 Are all natural fibers sustainable?

Not all natural fibers are sustainable, although most of them are renewable. Factors including production process, traceability, and working environment should be considered when deciding whether a fiber is sustainable.

13 What is the difference between regenerated and synthetic fibers?

Although both regenerated and synthetic fibers are chemically developed, regenerated fibers are derived from plants, and synthetic fibers are derived from chemicals.

14 What are the differences between polyester and nylon?

Nylon and polyester are both lightweight and durable synthetic fabrics that share many similar properties, such as wrinkle, stretch, and shrink resistance. Nylon is softer and stronger than polyester, while polyester is quicker to dry, has higher color fastness, and is abrasion resistant.

15 Do synthetic fibers come in different qualities?

The raw materials used to make synthetic fibers are more controllable than natural fibers, and therefore the quality of synthetic is more stable. However, production processes and finishings can still affect the outlook and characteristics of the fiber.

FUNCTIONS

16 Which fabrics are less likely to pill?

Aside from leather, all types of fabrics tend to pill over time. In general, long filament fibers do not pill unless they are snagged or broken. Short staple synthetic fibers (such as polyester) will eventually pill due to the accumulation of static electricity.

17 Which fabrics are best for dyeing?

Fabric made from wool, cotton, linen, silk, and nylon generally respond well to dyeing, but specific dyes can also help with fibers that normally do not react well.

18 Which fabrics are best for printing?

For transfer printing, polyester is the best option. The best material for printing is cotton because of its high absorbency.

19 Which fabrics are best for bleaching?

In general, fabrics made from natural fibers, such as cotton and linen, bleach better. With pre-treatment, stains and oils can be removed for a better dyeing, printing, or bleaching outcome.

20 Which fabric construction method will make a fabric more durable?

While fabric construction is not the only way to define the durability of a fabric, basket and twill weave tends to be more robust. They have less crimp and are flatter than plain weave. Fabrics made of basket and twill weave are often used for workwear, or other garments that require more durability.

21 Why are some fabrics more breathable or insulating than others?

The breathability and insulation of fabric depends on the fiber, thickness of the yarn, and weaving structure. Cotton is more breathable than polyester – thinner yarns and looser weaving allows air to pass through the fabric.

22

Why are some fabrics more transparent than others?

While the construction of transparent fabrics is the same as opaque fabrics, the use of thinner yarn, results in a sheerer fabric.

23

Why are some fabrics more absorbent than others?

Fiber content and construction defines the absorbency of fabric. Fabrics made from plants or animals are often able to absorb more liquid than synthetic fabrics, where weave construction, such as plain weave, can be less water repellent than dense twill weave. However, fiber type is the primary factor that determines absorbency, not the weave.

For more details on the absorbency of fibers, go to P.057.

24

What makes a fiber or fabric elastic?

Fiber choice and fabric construction are the two main factors that affect elasticity. In general, knitted fabric that contains spandex is the most elastic type of fabric.

For more details on the elasticity of fibers, go to P.057.

CARE AND MAINTENANCE

25

Are there any ways to prevent color fading?

Correctly washing and drying garments can prevent colors from fading. Some easy methods include turning clothes inside out and using a suitable detergent. Most importantly, read the care label and follow the washing instructions.

26

Why do white garments turn yellow when frequently washed?

White fabrics, especially synthetics, are usually finished with an optical whitening agent. This whitening agent can gradually wash away, causing fabrics to turn yellow. Detergent powder that contains optical whitener helps to maintain the whiteness of clothes for longer.

27

How can waterproof fabric be cleaned?

Depending on the care label, most waterproof jackets are machine washable. Other options include using a specific cleaner made for waterproof outerwear, or dry-cleaning. Alkaline-free detergent will not harm waterproof fabrics.

28

What are the differences between faux and real leather?

Real leather is made from animal hide, as opposed to faux leather, which is made with a plastic base and then treated with wax. The texture of real leather is unique and more durable, while faux leather has a more uniform texture, and can be worn more easily. They also differ in smell, fabric edges, and other characteristics.

For more details on real and faux leather, go to P.186.

FIBERS

Fibers are raw materials that can be converted into textile yarns and fabrics.

Fibers can be briefly classified into three types: natural, regenerated, and synthetic. Fibers are chosen for their specific properties, and can be used alone or combined depending on the desired properties.

(1.1) FIBERS CLASSIFICATION

NATURAL FIBERS

There are two main types:
- Animal (protein)
- Plant (cellulose)

Natural fibers are derived from either animals or plants, such as bast, skin, seeds, or shells

ANIMAL FIBERS

Wool

Cashmere

Qiviut

Vicuña

PLANT FIBERS

Cotton

Flax

Sisal

Abaca

REGENERATED (SEMI-SYNTHETIC) FIBERS

- Manufactured cellulosic fibers
- Manufactured protein fibers

Regenerated (semi-synthetic) fibers are derived from natural resources and go through an intensive chemical transformation process

PROTEIN FIBERS

Soybean Protein

Milk Casein

MANMADE FIBERS

Rayon

Acetate

SYNTHETIC FIBERS

Most polymers are similar to compounds that make up plastic, rubber, and coatings, and are developed through polymerization – a chemical process combining small molecules into polymers

SYNTHETIC FIBERS

Polyester

Nylon (Polyamide)

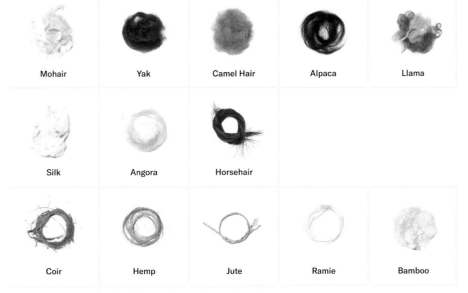

Mohair	Yak	Camel Hair	Alpaca	Llama
Silk	Angora	Horsehair		
Coir	Hemp	Jute	Ramie	Bamboo
Kapok				

Spandex	Olefin (Polypropylene PP)	Acrylic	Aramids	PVC (Polyvinyl Chloride)

COTTON (CO)

The most popular fiber
in the world.

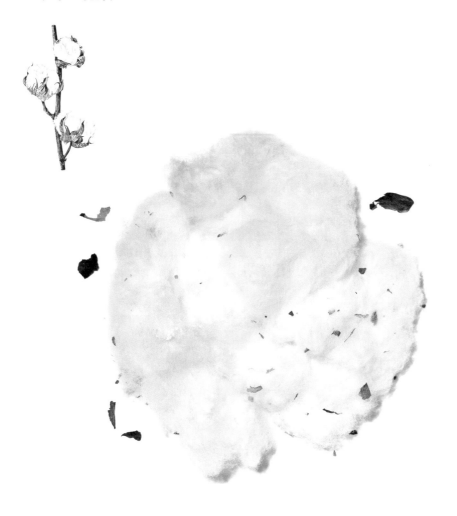

Wash in warm or
cool water

Machine washable

Can be air dried or
machine dried

Able to iron at a
high heat

DESCRIPTION

Cotton is a seed fiber grown as a protective case around the seed of the cotton plant. Known to be the most popular natural fiber in the world, it is soft and fluffy to the touch and is usually off-white in color.

STORY

Derived from the Arabic word "Kutan", cotton has been grown for more than 6000 years. First found woven in cloth around 3000 BC in Pakistan, it was then brought to Europe in about 800 AD by Arabic merchants, and by 1500 was known throughout the world.

MANUFACTURING

Conventional cotton requires extremely high moisture levels, resulting from rainfall or irrigation during the growing season, and a warm, dry season during the picking period. Picked cotton will go through ginning to separate the fibers from the seeds. Significant ecological and social impact caused by large-scale intensive production is a great concern in the industry.

POTENTIAL IMPACT

High global demand for cotton encourages large-scale intensive production. This requires a high usage of toxic chemicals and huge water consumption.

SEED FIBER

⊘ 11-22 microns
✎ 10-65 mm

CHARACTERISTICS

- Lightweight
- Durable, remains strong when wet
- Breathable and wearable all year round
- Absorbs and releases moisture very quickly
- Takes dye well but prone to discolor after wash
- Not stable and tends to shrink
- Prone to wrinkle
- Does not gather static electricity

CLASS OF COTTON

The grade of cotton depends on cleanliness, whiteness, fiber length, and fiber strength, but a longer staple usually indicates higher quality with a smoother hand feel.

STAPLE	LENGTH	CHARACTERISTICS
Extra Long	>35mm	Thin, long. smooth, soft, and glossy
Long	30-65mm	Smooth and soft
Medium	20-30mm	More abundant
Short	<20mm	Thick, short, coarse

EXTRA LONG STAPLE

Supima from America, Sea Island cotton from the Caribbean, and Giza cotton from Egypt are cottons with the highest qualities. They are all extra-long staple and very soft to the touch.

SUSTAINABLE OPTIONS

Organic cotton and color cotton are some sustainable options that have been promoted to replace conventional cotton, with fewer synthetic agricultural chemicals and less water usage.

FLAX Ⓛⓘ

A sustainable fiber
that produces
linen fabric.

DESCRIPTION

Flax is one of the oldest and strongest natural bast fibers and is extracted from flax or linseed plants. It is a stiff, crisp fiber with a natural luster. Its color usually ranges from ivory to light tan to gray.

HISTORY

Flax first dates back to being used in a linen headpiece in Israel 8500 years ago. Roughly 5000 years ago, both the Swiss and ancient Egyptians used flax to produce linen fabric. Linen was also used to wrap mummies in ancient Egyptian tombs.

Linen mummy-cloth

BAST FIBER

- ⊘ 12-16 microns
- ✎ 25-150 mm

CHARACTERISTICS

- Slightly silky and lustrous
- Durable, stiff, and crisp
- Withstands high temperatures
- Breathable and cool to wear in summer
- Low elasticity
- Pill and insect resistant
- Absorbs and releases moisture very quickly
- Fades under continuous sunlight
- Hard to achieve vivid colors as it is difficult to dye and bleach
- Softens and weakens after wash and wear
- Prone to wrinkle
- Anti-static
- Biodegradable

SUSTAINABLE BENEFIT

Flax is grown quickly and easily, requires few chemicals, and does not require irrigation during its cultivation.

Machine wash white and bright linen at any temperature

Do not bleach colored linen

Tumble dry with regular settings

Wash dark-colored linen with a lower temperature to prevent fading

Iron on high temperature settings

HEMP (CA/HA)
An important fiber for sustainable textiles.

DESCRIPTION

Hemp is a natural plant fiber extracted from the bast of Cannabis sativa. It is often considered as a "super fiber". True hemp is fine, light-colored and lustrous. It is naturally one of the most environmentally friendly fibers. Fine-quality hemp fabrics can be compared to linen. It is also used to blend with other fibers to improve its touch.

HISTORY

Hemp is one of the oldest known fibers, and was discovered in a tomb in Colombia dating back to 8000 BC. In early Asian and Middle Eastern civilizations, hemp was used in various applications. It also played a significant role in England in the 16th century; King Henry VIII even published a law that fined farmers who failed to grow the crop. It has been used in textiles for at least 6000 years.

BAST FIBER

⌀ 16-50 microns
✎ 15-25 mm

CHARACTERISTICS

- 8 times stronger than cotton
- Strength increases when wet
- Breathable and cool to wear in summer
- UV resistant
- Mildew and insect resistant
- Hypoallergenic, does not irritate skin but can be scratchy
- Hard to dye with high lignin content
- Softens after wash and wear
- Prone to wrinkle
- Biodegradable and renewable

SUSTAINABLE BENEFITS

A rapidly renewable fiber that can grow up to 4 meters in just 3 months. It only requires few chemical inputs and is highly adaptable to various climate conditions.

POTENTIAL IMPACT

Retting, the extraction process of hemp fibers from stems, produces wastewater that can be harmful to aquatic ecosystems.

Hand wash with cool water

Wash separately to avoid color running

Air dry or flat dry

(ALTERNATIVE)
Flax P.020, Jute P.022

JUTE ⓙⓤ

A low-cost, low-maintenance, and fast-growing fiber.

DESCRIPTION

Jute is a highly lignified natural plant fiber that is extracted from the Corchorus plant. It is also known as the "golden fiber" as it is generally golden-brown in color with a natural luster. It is second only to cotton when it comes to production and global consumption, as well as being one of the most affordable fibers.

HISTORY

Jute originated in India and has been grown on farms for centuries. The fiber started to be exported in the 1880s when a system for spinning and weaving was developed in Dundee, Scotland, which now has a jute museum. Jute products were replaced by synthetic fibers in the 1970s, and by the late 1990s, bulk packaging reduced the need for jute sacks.

Jute bag

BAST FIBER

⊘ 15-20 microns

CHARACTERISTICS

- Durable
- Strength decreases when wet
- Holds garment shapes well
- Low elasticity
- Able to insulate sound and heat
- Takes dye well and is colorfast
- Anti-static
- Biodegradable

SUSTAINABLE BENEFIT

It is a fast-growing and low-maintenance crop that can be harvested every 4 to 6 months and requires little use of pesticides or fertilizers.

POTENTIAL IMPACT

Retting, the extraction process of jute fibers from stems, produces wastewater that can be harmful to aquatic ecosystems.

Hand wash with cold water

Avoid twisting and squeezing

Air dry

Iron with a damp cloth

ALTERNATIVE
Flax P.020, Hemp P.021

RAMIE (RA)

A strong plant fiber that is similar to linen.

DESCRIPTION

Ramie, also commonly known as China grass or rhea, is one of the oldest fibers cultivated for textiles. It is also one of the strongest natural plant fibers. Naturally white in color and with silk-like luster, it is similar to linen. To improve its properties, it can also be blended with other fibers including cotton, polyester, and wool.

HISTORY

Ramie has been used since prehistoric times in China, India, and Indonesia. It was used in ancient Egypt and known in Europe during the Middle Ages. The usage of ramie increased in the mid-1980s due to a renewed interest in natural fibers.

BAST FIBER

⊘ 25-30 microns

CHARACTERISTICS

- Stiff and brittle, but softens with age and washing
- Strength increases when wet
- Holds garment shapes well
- Increases in silkiness after washing
- Withstands high temperatures
- Low elasticity
- Releases moisture quickly
- More absorbent than cotton
- Antibacterial and mold resistant
- Takes dye well but is prone to discolor and crock
- Tends to shrink slightly
- Prone to wrinkle and break when sharply creased
- Easily gathers static electricity

Wash at any temperature

Air or machine dry at a low temperature

Iron with a medium to high heat setting

(ALTERNATIVE)

Flax P.020, Silk P.040, Rayon P.046

BAMBOO (BB)

A very strong plant fiber with outstanding biodegradability.

DESCRIPTION

Bamboo is a natural bast fiber obtained from the pulp of bamboo plants. It can be processed into two major types of fiber: bamboo linen and bamboo viscose, which is the method used for the majority of bamboo fabric. Bamboo fiber is usually blended with other materials to make fabric.

HISTORY

Bamboo fiber originated in China, and was mainly used to make paper. Historically, it was also used for structural elements, such as bustles and the ribs of corsets. In the 20th century, the popularity of bamboo within the clothing industry grew, especially because of its environmental friendliness.

SUSTAINABLE BENEFIT

Bamboo is a rapidly renewable and biodegradable resource. It is a low-maintenance crop, requires few chemicals during cultivation.

BAST FIBER

⊘ 14-27 microns
✎ 1-5 mm

(ALTERNATIVE)
Cotton P.018, Cashmere P.029, Wool P.030, Polyester P.047

CHARACTERISTICS

- Lightweight, silky and soft
- Durable
- Highly breathable, and cool to wear in summer
- High elasticity
- Absorbs and releases moisture very quickly
- UV resistant
- Anti-bacterial and fungal resistant due to the bio-agent "bamboo kun*"
- Hypoallergenic
- Wrinkle resistant
- Anti-static
- Biodegradable

*Bamboo Kun is an anti-microbial bio-agent, which makes bamboo resistant to pests and fungi infestations.

POTENTIAL IMPACT

Chemical retting, which is the extraction process of bamboo fibers from stems, can produce wastewater that can harm aquatic ecosystems.

Hand or machine wash with gentle cycle

Avoid dry clean

Do not bleach

Line dry or machine dry with cool settings

SISAL Ⓢ

A strong, coarse fiber often used for ropes.

DESCRIPTION

Sisal is a natural fiber obtained from the leaves of the sisal plant. It is a hard and long fiber, where the leaves are beaten to separate tough fibers from the weak. The fiber has a coarse texture with lustrous, creamy white colors.

HISTORY

The sisal plant is native to Mexico, where its fiber has been extracted since pre-Columbian times. Commercial interest in sisal was stimulated by the development of the machine grain binder in the 1880s, which brought a demand for low-cost twine made out of sisal. Sisal twine and rope remains popular today due to its great strength.

LEAF FIBER

⊘ 200-400 microns
✎ 800-1000 mm

CHARACTERISTICS

- Coarse and lustrous
- Durable
- Water resistant, resistant to saltwater damage
- Able to insulate sound
- Takes dyes well but prone to discolor
- Abrasion resistant
- Biodegradable

QUALITY

Sisal can be divided into 3 basic gradings:

	COLOR	APPEARANCE
BEST	White, Soft Cream, Brown	Without knots
MEDIUM	Cream, Golden	Without knots and a medium amount of impurities
REJECTED	Brownish green	Presence of knots and a high percentage of impurities

Dry clean

Avoid exposure to water

ABACA

A low-cost and renewable fiber that can achieve a silk-like texture.

DESCRIPTION

Abaca, also known as Manila hemp, is extracted from the leaf sheath around the trunk of the abaca plant (also known as Musa textilis). A close relative of the banana tree, it is considered among the strongest natural fibers, and is usually up to 3 meters long. The best grades of the fiber are fine, lustrous, and light beige in color. Cellulose abaca fibers are relatively smooth and straight.

HISTORY

Ships rigging

Native to the Philippines, the abaca plant has been used for centuries. It was introduced to the West during the Spanish colonial period. During World War II, production in the Philippines declined, while production increased in the United States. Abaca was widely used for rigging ships and its pulp was used to make sturdy Manila envelopes at that time. Aklan, a province in the Philippines, produces the highest quality fiber of this type.

CHARACTERISTICS

- Lightweight and buoyant
- Soft and lustrous
- High elasticity, tensility and resilience
- Water and grease repellent
- Resistant to saltwater damage
- Takes dye well and is colorfast
- Renewable

BAST FIBER

✎ Up to 3000mm

Hand wash

Avoid dry-clean

Do not bleach

Dry flat

Iron under 150°C

(ALTERNATIVE)
Flax P.020, Hemp P.021, Jute P.022

KAPOK (KP)

A renewable, natural plant fiber often referred to as *"poor man's silk"*.

DESCRIPTION

Kapok is a natural cellulose plant fiber obtained from the fruit of the kapok tree, or the tree itself. It is sometimes referred to as Java cotton, ceiba, Java kapok, or silk cotton. The color ranges from white, pale yellow, to light brown, and consists of silky and lustrous textures. It is often blended with other fibers.

HISTORY

Kapok originated in South America and Africa. By the late 19th century, it became an important crop in Asia. With rising global wealth in the late Victorian era, the trend towards "overstuffed" sofas began. As kapok fibers were much cheaper than horsehair – the standard upholstery material used at the time – demand grew rapidly. Kapok was replaced by cheaper manmade substitutes after World War II but has recently made a comeback as organic and natural fibers have risen in popularity.

CHARACTERISTICS

- Very lightweight - 8 times lighter than cotton
- Soft, silky and oily
- Buoyant - 5 times more so than cork
- Brittle
- Water repellent
- Highly flammable
- Anti-microbial due to its natural bitter components
- Able to insulate sound
- Hypoallergenic
- Absorbs oils and dyes well
- Biodegradable and renewable

LINT FIBER

⊘ 30-36 microns
✎ 20-40 mm

Hand wash

Dry flat

Iron under 110°C

Avoid perchloroethylene during dry cleaning

COIR (CC)

A fiber extracted from coconut husk, often used for doormats.

DESCRIPTION

Coir is a highly lignified plant fiber extracted from coconut husk. It is the thickest and most resistant of all commercial natural fibers and is generally gold in color. There are two types of coir: the more commonly used brown fiber obtained from mature coconuts, and finer white fiber extracted from unripe green coconuts.

HISTORY

Originating in India, coconuts were first documented in the 3rd century BC. Ropes and cords have been made from coconut fiber since ancient times. Indian navigators who sailed the seas centuries ago used coir for ropes on their ships. During 1840, Treloar and Sons, a carpet manufacturer, began using coir fiber for various applications.

HARD FIBER

⊘ 12-25 microns
✎ Up to 350 mm

CHARACTERISTICS

- Coarse
- Durable and thick
- Able to insulate heat
- Retains moisture
- Waterproof, resistant to saltwater damage
- Flame and UV resistant
- Antibacterial; fungi and insect resistant
- Able to insulate sound
- Hard to dye due to its high lignin content
- Anti-static

COMMON TYPES

TYPES	APPEARANCE
Mature coconuts	Brown & rough
Unripe green coconuts	White & fine

(ALTERNATIVE)
Hemp P.021

Store in a cool, dry place

Avoid chemical treatment

Keep away from insects

CASHMERE (WS)

A softer, finer, and more luxurious wool fiber collected from goat.

DESCRIPTION

Cashmere is collected only from the undercoat of the Cashmere goat. Low in luster, the fiber is generally gray, brown, and white. Due to its rare production, the fiber alone is considered very luxurious, and is sometimes mixed with very soft wool.

HISTORY

The name cashmere comes from an old spelling of Kashmir – the region where its production and trade originated. The origin of these fibers dates back as far as the Mongolian empire in the 13th century. The Silk Road helped the development of cashmere, and shawls made of this fabric reached their greatest popularity in the early 19th century.

ANIMAL FIBER

⊘ 7-19 microns

✎ 25-90 mm

CHARACTERISTICS

- Silky and extremely fine
- Soft; drapes with a graceful flow
- Retains warmth and is comfortable to wear
- Weaker than wool and mohair
- Delicate and prone to pilling and abrasion
- Absorbs and retains moisture like wool
- Flame resistant
- Hypoallergenic
- Takes dye well
- Anti-static

BEST QUALITY

The best quality cashmere is between 13–15 microns in diameter and 35–37 mm.

ALTERNATIVE

Wool P.030, Mohair P.032, Yak P.033, Alpaca P.035, Camel P.034, Qiviut P.037, Vicuña P.036

Dry clean or hand wash with cool water

Steam at a low heat of 140°C

WOOL (WO)

A winter fiber commonly used in
suits and knit fabrics.

Dry clean and avoid
machine and hot
water washing

Do not use
chlorine bleach

Dry flat

Steam or press on a
medium heat setting
with damp cloth

DESCRIPTION

Wool is a natural protein fiber obtained from sheep, and there are over 200 different breeds worldwide. It is naturally crimped and wavy with a lofty and slightly greasy hand feel before treated. Most wools are yellowish white or ivory but some can be black, brown, gray, or random mixes.

HISTORY

Sheep are the oldest domestic animal species, dating back to around 10,000 years ago when primitive humans first covered their bodies with wool for protection. Britain's wool manufacturing industry is believed to be a leader in Europe around 1900 BC, and the death penalty was once effective for the exportation of sheep and raw wool during the 15th to 18th centuries. The first Merino sheep were introduced into Australia in 1797, where the best merinos continue to be bred to this day.

ANIMAL FIBER

⊘ 10-50 microns
✎ 40-115mm

GROWING

Wool fibers are obtained by sheep shearing that usually occurs in spring or early summer. The quality is determined by wool classing. The fleece is then treated with chemicals to remove "wool greases" and pests, and bleaching is often needed for white wool.

SUSTAINABLE OPTIONS

A sustainable approach includes encouraging the use of recycled wool and vegan wool.

BREEDS	DIAMETER
ULTRAFINE	<26 microns, 63.5-127mm e.g. Merino
FINE CROSSBRED	27-31 microns, 76.2-152.4mm e.g. Rambouillet, Blue Faced Leicester, Corriedales
MEDIUM CROSSBRED	23-34 microns, 76.2-152.4mm e.g. Columbia, Targhee, Finnsheep, Suffolk
COARSE CROSSBRED	>36 microns, 5-10 inches e.g. Lincoln

CHARACTERISTICS

- Weaker than cotton and flax
- Strength decreases when wet
- Holds garment shapes well
- Retains air and warmth
- High elasticity; considered the most extensible natural fiber
- Absorbs moisture better than cotton
- Fades and weakens under continuous sunlight
- Mildew develops when wool is damp
- Possible irritant to skin
- Trends to shrink when wet
- Scales make it possible to be felted
- Wrinkle resistant
- Biodegradable
- Suitable for mechanical recycling with relativity long fibers

COMMON TYPES OF WOOL

Wool fiber of different lengths is used to create different types of wool fabric. There is woolen fabric made with shorter wool fiber, and worsted fabric made with longer fiber, which is more tightly woven.

WOOLEN	WORSTED
Spun from wool fibers of: ✎ Short fibers of 25.4-76.2mm ⊘ Medium or coarse	Spun from wool fibers of: ✎ Longer than 76.2mm ⊘ Fine diameter
Fabric Appearance: Soft and fuzzy	Fabric Appearance: Crisp and smooth
Characteristics: • Insulator due to trapped air • Does not hold a crease well • Less durable than worsted	Characteristics: • Less insulating • Holds creases and shape • More durable than woolens

QUALITY OF WOOL

The quality of wool is determined by its fiber diameter, breed, amount of crimp, color, and staple strength. Fiber diameter is the most important wool characteristic when it comes to quality and price.

POTENTIAL IMPACTS

Treating methods for fly strike in sheep can constitute animal cruelty. And the treatment process of raw wool generally involves large amounts of chemicals and an intensive use of energy.

MOHAIR (WM)

A long, lustrous, and warm fiber that was once used to make garments for kings.

DESCRIPTION

Mohair is a silk-like fiber from the hair of the Angora goat. A long, white fiber that is notable for its high sheen and smooth feel, it is considered a luxury fiber like silk and cashmere, and has been given the nickname "diamond fiber". It is often blended with other fibers, especially wool.

STORY

Mohair is one of the oldest fibers in the world. The word mohair is derived from the Arabic word "mukhayyar", which means "finest fleece selected". The Angora goat was thought to originate from the mountains of Tibet and reached Turkey in the 16th century. It was later introduced to England, South Africa, and the United States in the 1800s. Mohair was popular as a wool-blend suiting fabric in the 1960s.

ANIMAL FIBER

⊘ 18-45 microns
✎ 100 to 150mm (sheared twice per year)
✎ 200 to 300mm (sheared once per year)

(ALTERNATIVE)
Cashmere P.029, Wool P.030,
Alpaca P.035, Angora P.039

CHARACTERISTICS

- Natural sheen due to the reflection of large outer fiber scales
- Most durable of all animal fibers
- High elasticity
- Absorbs and releases moisture
- Flame resistant
- Sheds dust and dirt more easily than wool
- Does not fade easily
- Takes dye exceptionally well
- Felts and shrinks less than wool
- Wrinkle resistant
- Biodegradable

BEST QUALITY

The length and quality of mohair depends on the number of shearing per year. Fewer shearing and younger Angora goats can produce finer, longer, and softer fibers that are considered higher quality (usually 19–20 microns) compared to adult mohair fiber.

Wash with cool water | Dry flat | Do not tumble dry | Spruce up by lightly shaking or brushing the fabric

YAK (WY)

A versatile and sustainable alternative to cashmere, which is highly valued in the Himalayas.

DESCRIPTION

Yak fiber is produced from the coat of yaks, a long-haired bovine known as "hairy cattle" in China. There are two layers of yak hair, naturally ranging from brown to black in color. The fine yak fibers are considered warmer than merino, as soft as cashmere and as tough as camel.

HISTORY

In the 1800s, there were numerous yaks in Tibet, but after 1900 they were hunted almost to extinction. They are also considered a vulnerable species because of interbreeding with domestic cattle. It has made a welcome addition to a marketplace that is growing weary of cashmere.

ANIMAL FIBER

⊘ 16-90 microns
✎ 25-150 mm

CHARACTERISTICS

- Soft
- Shiny, more lustrous than wool
- Retains warmth, and is 10-15% warmer than wool

QUALITY

OUTER FIBERS	79-90 microns	The outer fibers of a yak's coat are strong but coarse to the touch.
MIDDLE FIBERS	20-50 microns	Naturally strong, but not stronger than the outer layer fibers, and not as fine as the down fibers.
DOWN FIBERS	16-20 microns	The inner layer yields premium fine down fibers that are soft and warm to the touch.

Hand wash in cool water with mild soap or dry clean

Do not tumble dry

Remove excess water carefully without twisting

Avoid direct sunlight when drying

(ALTERNATIVE)
Cashmere P.029

CAMEL HAIR ⓌⓀ
A natural fiber worn by
native desert travelers
to protect themselves
from heat.

DESCRIPTION

A natural animal hair fiber, this specialty hair is
usually a golden tan shade. The fibers consist
of two parts: outer guard hair and an undercoat.
Outer guard hair is straighter and coarser, while
the undercoat is soft and fine. Baby camel is a
suitable alternative to cashmere.

HISTORY

The Bible contains the first reference to
camel hair; it mentions the material being
used for tents, carpets, and cloaks. Camel
hair was first used in fashion clothing by
Jaeger for coats and suits.

ANIMAL FIBER

- ⊘ 5-40 microns
- ✎ 380 mm, more (outer)
- ✎ 35-120 mm (inner)

CHARACTERISTICS

- Lightweight, smooth and soft
- Lustrous
- Excellent insulating properties
- Low elasticity, less so than wool
- More sensitive to chemicals than wool
- Takes natural dyes well
- Hard to put through the felting process

GRADES OF UNDERCOAT CAMEL HAIR

GRADE	APPEARANCE
FIRST	Fine, soft, and light tan in color
SECOND	Rougher to the touch, and often needs to be blended with sheep wool
THIRD	Ranging from brownish-black to tan; quite coarse and long

Dry clean or hand wash
with cool water

(ALTERNATIVE)
Cashmere P.029, Wool P.030, Alpaca P.035, Llama P.036

ALPACA (WP)
A rare, natural animal fiber that is softer than cashmere.

DESCRIPTION

Alpaca is a natural animal fiber from the South American camelid family. Its fiber is considered premium due to being light, fine, and warm. The fiber comes in a huge variety of colors from white to light brown, dark brown, and gray. It is also relatively rare to find on the market and is often blended with cashmere, mohair, and silk to improve softness and to make luxury clothing.

HISTORY

Alpacas were domesticated in the Andes Mountains region. Alpaca hair was reserved for making clothes for the royal family in the Incan Empire. Peruvians have also been wearing alpaca knits for centuries.

ANIMAL FIBER

⊘ 18-25 microns

CHARACTERISTICS

- Lightweight and very airy
- Very smooth and soft
- Felts readily, like wool
- Durable
- Retains warmth, and is 3-5 times warmer than wool
- Breathable and moisture wicking
- Flame resistant
- Hypoallergenic, does not irritate skin
- Takes dye well and is colorfast
- Wrinkle and pill resistant
- Slightly gathers static electricity

Wash with cold water and mild liquid detergent

Do not bleach

Avoid machine washing

(ALTERNATIVE)
Wool P.030, Mohair P.032, Llama P.036

LLAMA (WL)

An animal fiber that is similar to alpaca, but less fine and soft.

DESCRIPTION

Llama is a natural animal fiber from the South American camelid family. This fiber is similar to alpaca, but is thicker and less premium. Llamas have a double coat: a silky, wavy undercoat and a thicker, coarser outer coat. Generally, llama fibers are shades of brown, but can also contain specks of black and white.

HISTORY

Llamas are native to the Andes Mountains and were domesticated over 5000 years ago. European settlers adopted the name llama (also "lama" or "glama") from native Peruvians. Their popularity declined between the 11th and 13th centuries when they were selectively bred as load-carrying vehicles, and given the nickname "beasts of burden". Their rediscovery occurred in the 20th century.

UNDERCOAT FIBER

⊘ 20-25 microns
✎ 80-250 mm

CHARACTERISTICS (UNDERCOAT)

- Lightweight, hollow hair
- Soft and fine
- Straighter than most animal fibers
- Durable
- Difficult to process due to the diversity of fiber thickness
- Less elastic than alpaca fiber
- Weakens under continuous sunlight
- Oil and chemical resistant
- Hypoallergenic
- Shrinks easily and loses shapes when wet

Hand wash with cool water

Dry flat at room temperature

(ALTERNATIVE)
Wool P.030, Mohair P.032, Camel P.034, Alpaca P.035

QIVIUT

A rare, lightweight, and soft underwool fiber that is one of the finest natural fibers.

DESCRIPTION

Qiviut is the underneath wool fiber of the muskox, and is usually grayish-brown in color. For better quality, it can be spun into pure yarn or blended with merino, alpaca, cashmere, or silk. The price of qiviut fiber is high since its production volume is very limited.

HISTORY

Qiviut, meaning "muskox", originated in North America and Greenland. It was overhunted and reintroduced to Alaska in 1935. Qiviut fiber was first spun by an economics teacher in Alaska during the 1930s.

ANIMAL FIBER

⊘ 11-18 microns
✎ 35-70 mm

CHARACTERISTICS

- Soft
- Durable
- 8 times warmer than wool
- Drier than wool; contains about 7% oils
- Hypoallergenic, does not irritate skin
- Takes dye well
- Does not shrink or felt
- Odorless

VICUÑA (WG)
A rare, valuable, and delicate fiber made from vicuña.

DESCRIPTION

Vicuña is a silky, fine wool fiber from the undercoat of the vicuña. It is usually orange-brown in color or has natural colors.

STORY

In ancient times, vicuña fiber was known as the "Fiber of Gods". Only Incan royalty were permitted to wear it. The animals have been overhunted; therefore the species is classed as endangered and protected by the Peruvian and Bolivian governments. Loro Piana, LVMH-owned, is the only partner able to process and export vicuña textiles.

ANIMAL FIBER

⊘ 6-10 microns
✎ ~35mm

CHARACTERISTICS

- Softer and more delicate than cashmere
- Retains warmth
- Does not pill easily
- Able to shed moisture and dries quickly
- Flame resistant
- Hypoallergenic
- Easily damaged when dyed
- Biodegradable

Hand wash with warm water

Flat dry

(ALTERNATIVE)
Cashmere P.029

ANGORA (WA)

A soft animal fiber that has a floaty and fluffy feel.

DESCRIPTION

Angora is a fine and soft fiber of the Angora rabbit, which has very long and flexible hair. Various colors are available, including pure white, gray, brown, and black. Garments knitted from Angora fiber will feel like fur. It is also often blended with wool to enhance its elasticity.

ANIMAL FIBER

⊘ 11-14 microns

QUALITY

There are five grades of angora fiber; the lengths of fiber differ from its quality.

GRADE	APPEARANCE
FIRST (1A, 1B)	50.8-76.2mm, pure white fiber without impurities
SECOND	38.1-50.8mm waiver fiber
THIRD	25.4-38.1mm
FORTH	Mixed length
FIFTH	Any color; soiled, matted or unmatted

CHARACTERISTICS

- Lightweight, soft and silky
- Very thin, fine and fluffy with a halo effect
- Retains warmth; 100% Angora can be too warm to wear
- Very low elasticity
- Absorbs and releases moisture quickly
- Hard to dye
- Felts easily through abrasion
- Anti-static

Do not wring out

Hand wash with warm or cool water

Dry flat

(ALTERNATIVE)
Cashmere P.029, Wool P.030, Mohair P.032

SILK (SE)
One of the oldest known luxury natural fibers.

Hand wash with mild
soap or dry clean

Do not bleach

Hang to air dry

Iron with low heat,
inside out

DESCRIPTION

Silk is a very special natural fiber. Textile-used silk was often obtained from moth caterpillars. Long considered a luxury fiber, it is sometimes referred to as the "queen of fabrics". Silk is the only natural filament fiber and is soft, lustrous, shiny, and smooth to the touch.

ANIMAL FIBER

⊘ 10-13 microns
✎ From 500,000 to 1,500,000 mm

HISTORY

According to archeological evidence, silk has been used for at least 5000 years. According to Chinese legend, Empress Hsi Ling Shi, wife of the Yellow Emperor, sat under a mulberry tree and discovered that silkworm cocoons were made of a delicate thread. The Empress then learned how to make luxurious fabric by spinning the silk. It became very popular during the Han Dynasty, where silk became a currency that was traded.

MANUFACTURING

Silk can be produced by several insects, but the most common one is from caterpillar. Female moths lay 200-300 eggs over a couple of days and they grow from 2mm to 70mm in length during 25-30 days of non-stop eating. The silkworm starts to spin a cocoon of silk when it is fully grown, and one cocoon creates almost a mile of filament.

POTENTIAL IMPACT

The boiling of cocoons and the killing of the chrysalis to obtain the long silk filaments raises concerns over animal welfare concerns.

SUSTAINABLE OPTIONS

The use of wild (tussah) silk, ahimsa silk and organic silk are possible sustainable alternatives.

CHARACTERISTICS

- Smooth and drapes with a graceful flow
- One of the strongest natural fibers – stronger than cotton and linen
- Poor conductor of heat
- High elasticity
- Absorbs and releases moisture quickly
- Fades and weakens under continuous sunlight and sweat
- Sheds dust and dirt easily
- Takes dyes very well, and solid or vivid colors can be achieved
- Tends to shrink
- Wrinkle resistant
- Easily gathers static electricity

CULTIVATED AND WILD

The mulberry silkworm is the only cultivated silkworm, and also produces the best-quality silk.

	MULBERRY	TUSSAH	ERI	MUGA
🌐	CH	ID/CN/JP	TH/IN	IN
⊘	*****	***	*	****
◉	White	Deep Gold	-	Honey Gold

MOMME

Momme count (mm) is used to measure the density and strength of silk. The higher the number, the better the quality and the stronger the fabric. A silk fabric of 6 mm is a lightweight silk, while 22 mm is a heavyweight silk.

HORSE HAIR

A long, coarse hair obtained from the manes and tails of horses.

DESCRIPTION

Horse hair is an animal-protein fiber obtained from the manes and tails of horses. Hair from the mane is softer, while hair from the tail is coarser. Most horsehair comes from slaughtered horses, and is often black and lustrous.

HISTORY

The first documented use of horsehair was recorded in Switzerland during the 9th century as a blueprint plan, although some have said Spaniards were the first to use horsehair for textiles during the 8th century. It was used as interlining or stiffening for tailored garments and millinery, and became a popular upholstery and covering fabric for furniture during the 19th century.

Horsehair made interlining

ANIMAL FIBER

⊘ 50-150 microns (mane hair)
⊘ 75-280 microns (tail hair)

CHARACTERISTICS

- Lightweight, hollow
- Coarse and stiff
- Durable
- Heat resistant
- Can be felted but not as readily as wool
- Absorbs moisture slowly
- Antibacterial
- Takes dye well
- Biodegradeble

AGRICULTURE

Most horsehair comes from slaughtered horses.

MILK CASEIN
A regenerated fiber that resembles wool.

DESCRIPTION

Milk casein fiber is a regenerated animal-protein fiber obtained by the acid treatment of skimmed milk. The fiber is white, creamy, lustrous in color, and naturally crimped. It is usually blended with other fibers.

HISTORY

Milk casein dates back to the 14th century as a binder used for painting churches. Paint with casein applied to 14th- and 15th-century churches still appears bright and unfaded. Milk casein fiber originated in Italy, and was created by Antonio Ferretti in 1930.

CHARACTERISTICS

- Smoother and softer than wool, as it does not contain scales
- Chemically similar to wool
- Low durability; strength decreases when wet
- Excellent elasticity
- Absorbs moisture very quickly
- Similar flammability to wool, and becomes plastic and sticky when temperature is raised
- Easily damaged by mildew
- Same pH level as human skin
- Takes dye well
- Biodegradable

Able to dry-clean

Hand wash or machine wash gently with cool water

Do not bleach

Flat dry

Press with wool setting

ALTERNATIVE
Wool P.030, Silk P.040, Rayon P.045

SOYBEAN PROTEIN (SPF)

A sustainable alternative to silk also known as vegetable cashmere or *"silk for vegans"*.

DESCRIPTION

Soybean protein fiber (SPF) is also known as soy silk and vegetable cashmere. It is an environmentally friendly regenerated plant protein fiber made from soy pulp, which is the insoluble part of soybeans and also a by-product of tofu and soy milk production. It is usually golden in color and has a soft and smooth texture with a natural sheen. The fiber is usually blended with other fibers to increase drape and strength.

HISTORY

The manufacture of soybean fiber dates back to 1931, when Henry Ford hired chemists Robert Boyer and Frank Calvert to produce artificial silk. They succeed, and it was presented as Azlon. Henry Ford promoted the fiber by wearing a soy-fabric suit and necktie, as well as equipping Ford vehicles with soybean upholstery. Although it never reached the commercial market, being overtaken by nylon during World War II, it did made a comeback in 1998.

CHARACTERISTICS

- Smooth and soft
- Delicate, not as strong as other natural fibers
- Strength decreses when wet
- Retains warmth
- Stretchable
- Absorbs and releases moisture very quickly
- Antibacterial
- Takes dye well and is colorfast
- Shrink resistant
- Wrinkle resistant
- Biodegradable

Hand wash or gentle cycle with cold water

Hang or flat dry

Iron with a low heat setting without steam

ACETATE (AC)

A silky, soft semi-synthetic material that is often blended with other fibers.

DESCRIPTION

Acetate is one of the earliest semi-synthetic fibers. It is produced by treating wood pulp or cotton linters with acetate acid and acetylating hydroxyl groups. With a silky, soft texture and a lustrous sheen, it is commonly used as an alternative to silk. While it shares many similar properties to rayon, they differ in their production process. It is also commonly blended with other fibers.

HISTORY

First used in France as a varnish for aircraft, acetate was later developed as a fiber in Great Britain in 1923, and as a fabric in the United States in 1924. Certain fumes and pollutants caused the fabric to fade or discolor, meaning it was never mass-produced. While chemists managed to solve the discoloration problem, it still occurred when exposed to pollutants. Due to the rise of polyester fibers, which have better wash-and-wear properties, the production of acetate fibers has declined since the mid-20th century.

CHARACTERISTICS

- Smooth and soft
- Drapes with a graceful flow
- Highly breakable, especially when wet
- Heat sensitive and prone to melting
- Low elasticity
- Pill resistant
- Moisture wicking and fast drying
- Mildew and mold resistant
- Requires special dyes to be colorfast
- Prone to wrinkle, suitable for pleating
- Gathers static electricity

VARIATIONS

TRIACETATE: Contains a higher number of acetylated hydroxyl groups. More heat resistant but less absorbent than regular acetate.

Dry clean only

Avoid tumble dry

Iron with low heat setting using a damp cloth

RAYON

A versatile fiber
often referred to as
artificial silk.

DESCRIPTION

Rayon was the first manufactured semi-synthetic fiber. It blends well with other fibers to create fabrics that feel soft and silky. There are many varieties of rayon; they differ slightly in both the manufacturing process and properties of the finished product.

HISTORY

Invented in France during the 1890s, rayon was created to be an affordable imitation of silk, wool, cotton, and linen. It was originally called "viscose", which is still used in Europe today. In 1924, the North American textile industry adopted the term "rayon viscose".

CHARACTERISTICS

- Smooth and soft
- Silky and lustrous
- Highly breakable, especially when wet
- Absorbs moisture quickly
- Highly flammable
- Takes dye well
- Tends to shrink
- Prone to wrinkle

ALTERNATIVE

Cotton P.018, Bamboo P.024, Silk P.040

VARIATIONS

MODAL (MD) : A beechwood pulp fiber with a smoother surface and softer touch than rayon viscose. Durable, breathable, and shrink resistant, it is commonly used to produce lingerie and household products.

LYOCELL (LY/CLY) : A bleached wood pulp fiber with high tensibility and the ability to absorb moisture. It is stronger and more breathable than rayon viscose and also the most environmentally friendly option of all rayon variations. It is also an eco-silk alternative as it can be spun into long yarns that are silky and smooth. The fiber is often used for sportswear and lingerie.

CUPRO (CU) : A cotton linter regenerated fiber with a silky, smooth texture and a shiny surface. The fiber is anti-static, stretchable, and can regulate body temperature, which is why it is widely used as interfacing.

VISCOSE (VI) : Also known as viscose rayon, it is made from wood pulp or cotton linter and has a silky texture. However, its production process contributes to high levels of greenhouse gas emissions. Viscose can be less durable than other types of rayon.

Dry clean or hand
wash with cool water

Flat dry

POLYESTER (PL)

One of the world's most widely used fibers, often used for fast fashion.

DESCRIPTION

A synthetic fiber derived from petroleum, polyester is generally available in two types: polyethylene terephthalate (PET) and Poly-1, 4-cyclohexylene terephthalate (PCDT). PET, a stronger type of polyester, is more popular for clothing and is commonly blended with natural fibers. PCDT is more often used in furnishings due to its elastic and resilient properties.

Polyester-made plastic bottle

HISTORY

Terylene, the first polyester fiber, was created in Great Britain between 1931 and 1941. In 1956, the production rights were bought by an American company, DuPont, and renamed Dacron for the United States market. Praised for having zero wrinkles (even after washing), one of the fabric's earliest uses was for suiting.

CHARACTERISTICS

- Soft and drapes easily
- Holds garment shapes well
- Highly durable
- Retains pleats set by heat
- Pill resistant in filament form
- Fast drying
- Mildew and soil resistant
- Lower price-point than most fabrics
- Takes dye well, requires high-temperature dye

POTENTIAL IMPACT

Polyester is derived from nonrenewable petroleum and is manufactured using an energy-intensive and greenhouse gas-emitting process.

SUSTAINABLE OPTIONS

Mechanically and chemically recycled polyester and recycled polyester from PET bottles are more sustainable options.

Machine washable on a low temperature

Tumble dry with a low setting

Iron with low heat

NYLON (PA)

A stretchy fabric commonly used in hosiery and swimwear.

DESCRIPTION

Nylon, also called polyamide (PA), is derived from petroleum. The two most common types of nylon are nylon 6 and nylon 6.6. Originally created as a thermoplastic substitute for silk, it is one of the strongest fibers and is very elastic. It is often blended with other fibers to improve its properties.

HISTORY

Produced by Wallace Carothers at DuPont's research facility in 1935, nylon was the first commercially successful synthetic thermoplastic polymer. Initially used to create the bristles of toothbrushes in 1938, it went on to be used for stockings in 1940, and for military parachutes during World War II.

Military parachutes

CHARACTERISTICS

- Smooth and soft
- Extremely durable, even when wet
- Heat sensitive and prone to melt
- High elasticity
- Moisture wicking and fast drying
- Soil resistant
- Mildew and fungi resistant
- Takes dye well, but dark shades can fade during washing
- Wrinkle resistant
- Easily gathers static electricity

POTENTIAL IMPACT

Nylon is made from non-renewable resources, and an environmentally unfriendly, durable, water-repellent finishing is often applied to nylon garments or products.

SUSTAINABLE OPTIONS

Closed-loop, chemically recycled nylon is a more sustainable option.

Machine wash with cool or warm water

Wash separately to prevent colors from running

Avoid using chlorine bleach

Air dry or machine dry on the lowest temperature

Iron on a low heat

OLEFIN (PP/PE)
A strong, stain-resistant fiber often used for wallpaper.

DESCRIPTION

Olefin synthetic fibers are made from polyolefin – a term for colorless plastics that feel waxy and oily. The two most important strands are called polyethylene and polypropylene, with polypropylene being more commonly used in the textile industry.

HISTORY

Olefin fibers were first produced in Italy during 1957 by Nobel Prize winners Giulio Natta and Karl Ziegler, to increase the number of textile applications. The United States also started producing olefin in 1960.

POTENTIAL IMPACT

The manufacturing of olefin fibers requires non-renewable resources and high water and energy use.

CHARACTERISTICS

- Polyethylene (PE) is generally lighter
- Polyethylene (PE) is more stable in temperature
- Durable
- Buoyant, making it ideal for high-performance apparel
- Low melting temperature, especially polyethylene
- Pill resistant
- Moisture wicking and fast drying
- Stain resistant
- Cannot be dyed
- Lowest static among synthetic fiber
- Non-biodegradable

SUSTAINABLE OPTIONS

Sustainable approaches include recycled polyethylene and polypropylene.

Wash with cold or warm water

Avoid high temperatures

Tumble dry with little or no heat

Do not iron

SPANDEX (EL/EA)

An incredibly stretchy
fiber that is a key
component of
elastic fabrics.

DESCRIPTION

Spandex, also known as elastane, is
segmented polyurethane, and a by-product
of petroleum. It is a white-colored synthetic
fiber made to provide elasticity. The fiber
can stretch to over 500% of its length and
recover to its original length immediately. It
is often blended with other fibers to offer
additional stretch.

HISTORY

Spandex was developed in 1959 by DuPont
textile scientist Joseph C. Shivers as a
substitute for rubber. Originally called Fiber
K, DuPont chose the trade name Lycra®
to distinguish its brand of spandex fiber. It
was totally revolutionary, and was quickly
incorporated into swimwear, undergarments,
and other clothing.

POTENTIAL IMPACT

Spandex is made from nonrenewable
resources. Toxic solvents are used in its
production, and hazardous pollutants are
emitted into the air during the process.

CHARACTERISTICS

- Lightweight, smooth and soft
- Relatively weak as a fiber, but stronger and
  more durable than rubber
- Excellent elasticity
- Pill resistant
- Oil and perspiration resistant
- Mildew and insect resistant
- Takes dye well
- Wrinkle resistant
- Abrasion resistant
- Anti-static

SUSTAINABLE OPTIONS

The use of bio-based spandex is encouraged
as a sustainable option.

Machine washable

Avoid high temperature

Drip dry

ACRYLIC (PC)

A synthetic fiber that is similar to wool but more affordable.

DESCRIPTION

Acrylic fiber is made from a synthetic polymer called acrylonitrile. It is produced by reacting certain petroleum or coal-based chemicals with a variety of monomers. It has a wool-like aesthetic and can be used on its own or blended with other natural and synthetic fibers, which enhances its stretchiness, luster, and warmth.

HISTORY

Acrylic was created in 1941 by DuPont and trademarked as Orlon. However, it was not produced in large quantities commercially until the 1950s.

POTENTIAL IMPACT

Acrylic is not biodegradable or generally recycled. The processing of acrylic also involves emissions that include a high amount of volatile organic compounds.

CHARACTERISTICS

- Lightweight and soft
- Wear and tear resistant
- Retains warmth
- Prone to melt
- Pills easily and is often chemically treated
- Moisture wicking and fast drying
- Highly UV resistant
- Chemical resistant, stable with common bleaching agents
- Mildew and insect resistant
- Takes dye and is colorfast
- Washes easily and will not shrink like wool
- Gathers static electricity

Machine wash with cold water

Fabric softener recommend

Drip dry

Iron with low to medium heat

(ALTERNATIVE)

Wool P.030

PVC

A component used to make smooth and shiny fabric, commonly applied in punk and gothic clothing.

DESCRIPTION

PVC, sometimes referred to as vinyl or vinyon, is a synthetic resin made from the polymerization of vinyl chloride. It has a smooth, shiny plastic surface and is naturally white. It is often confused with patent leather.

HISTORY

PVC was first invented by Waldo Semon in 1931 to replace rubber – one of the earliest synthetic fibers. The first commercial use of the fiber was in 1939, and it grew in mainstream popularity in the 1950s and 1960s. PVC is prevalent in alternative clothing categories including goth, punk, and fetish.

Mary Quant raincoat from the 1960s

CHARACTERISTICS

- Highly durable
- Less heat resistant than polyester and nylon
- Tear resistant
- Water resistant
- Flame and UV resistant
- Chemical resistant
- Mildew and insect resistant
- Shrinks in hot water
- Gathers static electricity

Store at room temperature in a dry place

Wash with low to medium temperatures

Avoid softening agents

Tumble dry using medium temperatures or air dry

ARAMID

An exceptionally
strong fiber best known
for manufacturing
bulletproof vests.

DESCRIPTION

Aramid is a high-performance synthetic fiber
made from aromatic polyamide. There are two
types of aramid – Nomex, which is chemical,
electrical, and fire resistant; and Kevlar,
which is extremely strong and usually gold in
color. Aramid fibers can be very strong
yet lightweight.

HISTORY

The name aramid is a short for "aromatic
polyamide". Aramid was first created at
DuPont by Stephanie Kwolek during the
1930s. In the 1970s, it was used commercially
to replace steel in racing tires.

CHARACTERISTICS

- Lightweight and stiffer than glass
- Highly tear and cut resistant with excellent
  ballistic properties
- Flame resistant
- Sensitive to UV
- Chemical resistant but sensitive to acids
- Non-conductive

MICROFIBER
Ultra-thin synthetic fiber that is less than 1 denier.

DESCRIPTION

Microfiber commonly made from nylon, acrylic, and polyester, microfiber can vary in composition and combinations of synthetic fibers. Although they have a wide range of applications, they are somewhat controversial due to the fact that they are non-biodegradable and can damage the oceanic food chain.

HISTORY

Microfiber was invented in Japan during the 1970s to create lightweight, flattering swimwear for women. Unfortunately, it failed, as the swimsuits absorbed water and became very heavy. Europeans then redeveloped microfiber, with DuPont introducing the "first" microfiber made from polyester in 1989.

Cross-section of microfiber

CHARACTERISTICS

- Lightweight, soft and drapes easily
- Ultrafine; finer than the most delicate silk
- Insulates against wind, rain, and cold weather
- Absorbs moisture quickly with a split weave
- Shrink and stretch resistant

MANUFACTURING

Split Weave or Looped Weave: Water Absorbent — Split-weave microfiber is made by the fibers being split in production. Thousands of tiny loops are formed when the threads are split. This increases the surface area, which makes it more absorbent and able to pick up small dirt particles.

Flatweave: Water Repellent — Flatweave microfiber only has half the moisture-absorbing capabilities of split-weave microfiber, and repels water accordingly.

Wash in warm water with mild detergent

Avoid fabric softeners

Wash microfiber with microfiber, or with other lint-free fibers

Follow the instructions for washing different individual fibers

(1.2) BLENDED FIBERS

Fiber blends and mixed yarns are made by combining 2 or more textile fibers. When blended or mixed together, these fibers can modify or change the properties, as well as the appearance of fiber, yarn, or fabric. They utilize the characteristics of each kind of fiber and are used to help meet specific industry requirements.

BLENDED FIBERS		MIXED YARNS	
Combines 2 or more fiber substances into a single fiber strand.		Combines 2 or more strands of different fibers to form one yarn, which can be single or plied.	

Blended fibers and mixed-yarn fabrics are produced for the following reasons:

- To improve the appearance of a fabric, such as texture, color, and tone
- To improve the quality of a fabric, such as durability, strength, and texture
- To improve the ease of handling a fabric to be sewed, or to retain its shape
- To improve the profitability of fabric, making it cheaper to produce

COMMON TYPES OF BLENDS

WOOL NYLON + ACRYLIC BLEND	• Cheaper production • More durable	• Easier handling
COTTON + POLYESTER BLEND	• Cheaper production • Texture similar to cotton	• Resistant to shrinkage • Resistant to creases
SILK + POLYESTER BLEND	• Cheaper production	• Easier handling

PROCESS

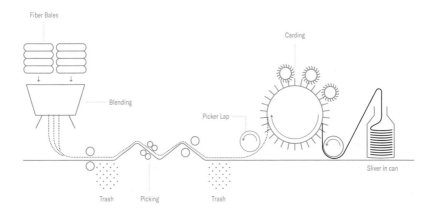

(1.3) FIBERS COMPARISON

FIBER		MAINTENANCE	ABRASION RESISTANCE	STRENGTH	DRAPABILITY
WOOL		****	**	*	*****
CASHMERE		*****	*	**	****
MOHAIR		****	*****	**	***
ALPACA		***	****	**	***
CAMEL		****	***	***	***
ANGORA		****	***	***	***
SILK		****	*****	****	*****
COTTON		***	*****	****	***
FLAX		**	*****	*****	***
RAMIE		**	*****	*****	***
ACETATE		****	*	***	*****
VISCOSE RAYON		****	**	**	*****
ACRYLIC		***	****	****	*****
POLYAMID (NYLON)		**	*****	*****	*
POLYESTER		**	*****	*****	****
POLYURETHANE (SPANDEX)		**	*****	*****	****

ELASTICITY	ABSORBENCY	SHRINKAGE	DYE ABSORPTION	ANTI-STATIC
*****	*****	*****	*	*
*****	*****	*****	*	*
*****	****	***	*	*
****	****	****	*	*
****	****	****	*	*
****	****	****	*	*
*****	*****	***	***	***
**	****	***	***	***
*	***	**	*****	***
*	****	**	*****	***
****	***	*	*****	***
*	****	***	**	***
****	***	***	***	***
*****	*	*	*****	*****
*****	*	*	*****	*****
*****	*	***	***	*

1.4 BURN TEST

Burning yarns or threads in the warp or weft direction indicates a fabric's content.

PLANT	EFFECT OF HEAT	EFFECT OF FLAME	ODOR & RESIDUE
COTTON	Scorches; does not burn until 246°C	Scorches; burns quickly; steady yellow flame	Burning paper; light and easily crushed gray ash
FLAX	Discolors; decomposes about 120°C	Scorches; burns quickly; bright yellow flame	Burning leaves or wood; light and gray ash
HEMP	No melted bead; loses weight between 100-150°C	Burns quickly; bright yellow flame	Burning leaves or wood; light and gray ash
RAMIE	Decomposes at 200°C	Scorches; burns quickly; steady yellow flame	Burning leaves or wood; light and easily crushed gray ash
JUTE / KENAF	Discolors; does not shrink; decomposes at about 120°C	Does not shrink from flame; yellow flame	Burning leaves or wood; light and gray ash
BAMBOO	/	Burns quickly and steady; yellow to orange flame	Burning paper; irregular easily crushed ash

SYNTHETIC	EFFECT OF HEAT	EFFECT OF FLAME	ODOR & RESIDUE
POLYESTER	Sticks at 227-230°C; melts at 246-260°C	Burns quickly and melts; shrinks; orange flame	Fruity chemical smell; black hard round bead
NYLON	Yellows at 150°C; melts at 215-250°C	Burns quickly; shrinks	Celery-like smell; hard, round, tough bead
OLEFIN	Shrinks and curls	Burns and melts	Asphalt; hard, tan bead
SPANDEX	Sticks at 180°C; melts at 230-290°C	Burns slowly and melts; does not shrink	Bitter and sharp odor; soft, sticky black ash
PVC	Shrinks at 70°C; decomposes at 180°C	Extinguishes; yellow flame with green spurts	Hydrochloric acid; plastic chars
ACRYLIC	Sticks to surface when pressed at 251-255°C	Burns quickly; shrinks; white-orange flame	Charred meat; irregular, hard crust
ARAMID	Shrinks	Puckers and chars	No smell; hard black bead

ANIMAL

	EFFECT OF HEAT	EFFECT OF FLAME	ODOR & RESIDUE
WOOL **MOHAIR** **CASHMERE** **CAMEL HAIR**	Curls; loses softness; slowly ignites; chars around 300°C	Burns slowly; orange flame; self-extinguishes	Burning hair or feathers; crisp, easily crushed ash
ALPACA **LLAMA**	Curls; loses softness; slowly ignites; chars around 300°C	Burns quick; orange flame; does not self-extinguish	Burning hair or feathers; crisp, easily crushed ash
SILK	Remains unaffected around 140°C; decomposes at 175°C	Burns and melts slowly; sizzles; ceases to flame	Burning hair or feathers; soft and easily crushed ash

MANMADE

	EFFECT OF HEAT	EFFECT OF FLAME	ODOR & RESIDUE
RAYON / VISCOSE	Does not melt; loses strength at 150°C; decomposes at 185-205°C	Scorches; burns readily and quickly; yellow flame	Burning paper; leaving little ash
MODAL / LYOCELL	Slowly ignites; color changes at 150°C	Burns slowly; dissolves	—
ACETATE	Sticky at 190°C; melts at 260°C	Burns and melts	Smells of vinegar; hard, irregular black ash

PROTEIN

	EFFECT OF HEAT	EFFECT OF FLAME	ODOR & RESIDUE
MILK CASEIN	Softens, becomes brittle, and yellows at 100°C; decomposes at 150°C	Burns slowly in air; orange flame; self-extinguishes	Smells like wool; crisp, easily crushed ash
SOYBEAN PROTEIN	Strength decreases; yellows at 160°C	Burns slowly in air; orange flame; self-extinguishes	Smells like burning protein fiber; easily crushed ash

— YARNS

Yarn is a long, continuous length of interlocked fibers.

There are two main types of yarn: staple yarn (also called spun yarn), made with shorter fibers, and filament yarn, made from long, continuous filament fibers. The yarn-spinning process that brings fibers together can be done by machine or hand, providing different qualities and creating different yarn structures. Factors such as the length of the fiber, yarn count, and twist direction can all contribute to the appearance, strength, and other properties of fabrics.

(2.1) STAPLE YARN

Staple or spun yarn is made from fibers that are short in length. Staple fibers must be spun or twisted together to make a long, continuous strand of yarn. Staple yarns can contain a single type of fiber or can be blended with various types of fibers – most commonly synthetic with natural fibers.

STAPLE SPINNING

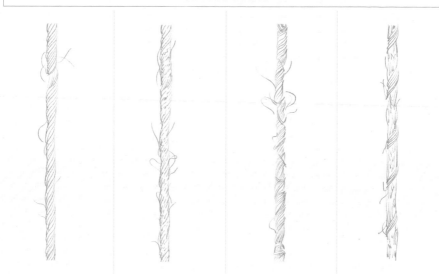

RING SPINNING	OPEN END FRICTION SPINNING	OPEN END ROTOR SPINNING	AIR JET SPINNING
Oldest spinning method	1970s and early 1980s	1970s and early 1980s	Early 1980s
Slivers are drafted into rovings and twisted into yarns before being wound onto the bobbin	Spun from slivers using spinning rotor with withdrawal system to create false twisted yarns	Spun from slivers using spinning rotor with withdrawal system to create false twisted yarns	Slivers are drafted and fed into a vortex created by high-speed air jets to create false twists
Results in strong yarn	Results in weak yarn	Results in weak yarn	Results in weak yarn
Finest yarn	Less well aligned yarn	Less well aligned yarn	Least well aligned yarn
Large range of yarn count	Small range of yarn count	Small range of yarn count	Small range of yarn count
Suitable for all staple fibers	Not suitable for manmade fibers, except rayon	Not suitable for manmade fibers, except rayon	Commonly used for producing polyester
Slowest production rate	Faster production rate than ring spinning	Faster production rate than ring spinning	Fastest production rate (20 times faster than ring spinning)
More steps required	Fewer steps needed	Fewer steps needed	Fewer steps needed

(2.2) FILAMENT YARN

Filament yarn is continuous in length. By forcing liquid or semi-liquid polymers through small holes, a single- or multiple-filament yarn is created. Filament yarns can be grouped into bundles, and cut into desired staple lengths. Silk is the only natural filament yarn.

FILAMENT SPINNING		

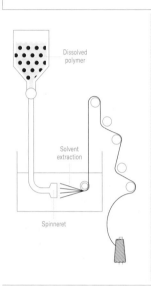 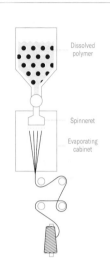 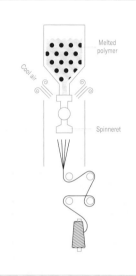

WET SPINNING	DRY SPINNING	MELT SPINNING
Polymers are dissolved in a solvent and extruded directly into a liquid bath	Polymers are dissolved in a volatile solvent that evaporates when extruded	Polymer granules are melted and then extruded through the spin head
Viscose rayon, acrylic, aramid, spandex	Acetate, acrylic	Polyester, nylon
Low investment cost	High investment cost	Low investment cost
Small amount of yarn production	Small amount of yarn production	Larger amount of yarn production
Toxic production process	Toxic production process, risk of explosion	Non-toxic production process
Slow production rate	Fast production rate	Fastest production rate

(2.3) PROCESSING YARN

CARDED
A low-cost yarn-production process creating fuzzy yarn for lightweight fabric

COMBED
A more expensive yarn production process creating smoother and softer yarn. This method includes carding and additional processes that produce more waste

	CARDED	COMBED
FIBER	Cotton, waste silk, plant fiber, hair or wool fibers, and synthetic staple fibers	Fine cotton and all fibers after carding
LENGTH OF FIBER	Short, medium and long fibers	Long-staple fibers
CHARACTERISTICS	• Non-uniform • Usually coarser to the touch • Easily shrunk	• Straight and aligned fiber • Soft and smooth to the touch • Lustrous in appearance

WOOLEN
Woolen threads are uneven fibers made from carded and uneven fibers.

WORSTED
Worsted yarns are combed wool yarns made from parallel wool fibers.

	WOOLEN	WORSTED
LENGTH OF FIBER	25.4-76.2mm short fibers	76.2mm or above long staple fibers
CHARACTERISTICS	• Bulky and uneven • Slackly twisted • Soft and hairy	• Fine and even • Tightly twisted • Soft and hairy

⦅2.4⦆ YARN SYSTEM

What to Consider in One Yarn :
Fineness of the yarn – the finer the count, the smoother the hand feel and the higher the price. Two types of systems are used: direct (mass/length) and indirect (length / mass).

DIRECT SYSTEM

The higher the count, the coarser the yarn. The yarn count measures the number of weight units in one length unit.

GENERALLY USED
Synthetic, Jute, Silk

COMMON SYSTEM
- Denier
- Tex
- Deci-Tex
- Pound per spindle (Jute Count)

High Yarn Count Low Yarn Count

DENIER (TD)

The number or count in the denier system is the weight in grams of 9000m.

$$\frac{\text{⟨o⟩ (gm)}}{1\ gm} \times \frac{9000\ m}{\text{(m)}}$$

TEX (TEX)

Defined as the weight in grams of 1000m.

$$\frac{\text{⟨o⟩ (gm)}}{1\ gm} \times \frac{1000\ m}{\text{(m)}}$$

INDIRECT SYSTEM

The higher the count, the finer the yarn. The yarn count measures the number of length units in one weight unit.

GENERALLY USED
Cotton, Worsted, Woolen
Flax (wet spun)

COMMON SYSTEM
- English Cotton Count
- Metric Count
- Worsted Count
- Woolen Count

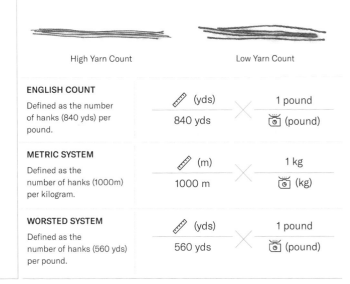

High Yarn Count Low Yarn Count

ENGLISH COUNT

Defined as the number of hanks (840 yds) per pound.

$$\frac{\text{(yds)}}{840\ yds} \times \frac{1\ pound}{\text{⟨o⟩ (pound)}}$$

METRIC SYSTEM

Defined as the number of hanks (1000m) per kilogram.

$$\frac{\text{(m)}}{1000\ m} \times \frac{1\ kg}{\text{⟨o⟩ (kg)}}$$

WORSTED SYSTEM

Defined as the number of hanks (560 yds) per pound.

$$\frac{\text{(yds)}}{560\ yds} \times \frac{1\ pound}{\text{⟨o⟩ (pound)}}$$

⟨o⟩ = WEIGHT

⟨✎⟩ = LENGTH

(2.5) PLY YARN

While all yarns are originally spun as a single yarn, they may be twisted together to produce a "ply yarn" for different end uses. One of the most commonly produced yarns is 2-ply yarn, which is formed by twisting 2 single yarns together with the ply twist opposite to the direction of the yarn twist. Yarns with a higher ply number can create stronger and less wrinkly fabrics.

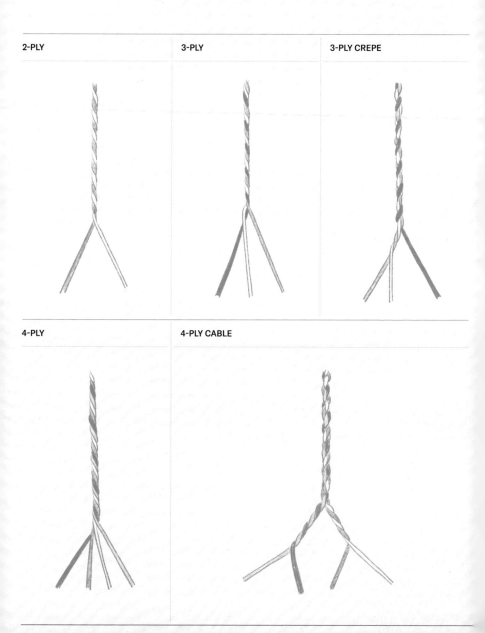

2-PLY

3-PLY

3-PLY CREPE

4-PLY

4-PLY CABLE

2.6 YARN TWIST

Yarn twists are used to capture fibers and secure them. They will influence different properties of yarn.

DIRECTION

The direction of twist affects the light reflection and the appearance of a fabric. Twist directions are described as either an "S" or "Z" twist; most spun yarn has a "Z" twist. Twist direction does not influence the properties of single yarn, and the ply twist direction is generally opposite to the twist of the yarn. Smooth fabrics tend to stick with the one yarn twist direction and stick to another ply twist direction. Fabric with texture effects tends to have mixed directions.

S TWIST — Thread appears to move upwards towards the left yarn

Z TWIST — Thread appears to move upwards towards the right yarn

LEVEL

The twist level is determined by the number of turns present in a unit of yarn length. High-twist yarn has a higher number of twists within the same unit length when compared to a low-twist yarn. For example, the twist number determines the yarn's strength, elongation characteristics, and air permeability. Yarn used for weaving tends to have a high twist, resulting in smooth surfaces and higher lengthwise strength. Yarn used for knitting has a looser twist.

LOW TWIST — Used to make bulky, soft, and fuzzy fabrics

HIGH TWIST — Used to make smoother surfaces and denser fabrics

2.7 COMPLEX YARN & TEXTURE YARN

COMPLEX YARN

Complex yarns, sometimes referred to as novelty yarns, are single or plied yarn structures with irregularities. Used to make fabrics more interesting, these irregularities can relate to size, twist effect, or color. For example, yarns that are thicker, thinner, or have curls, loops, or twists.

SLUB YARN

SPIRAL YARN

BOUCLÉ YARN

LOOP YARN

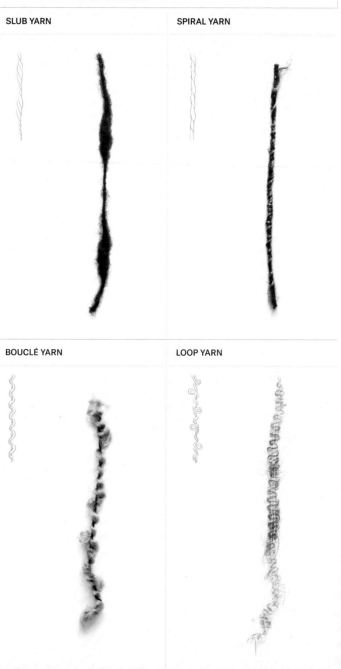

SNARL YARN

KNOP YARN

CHENILLE YARN

TWEED

[2.7] COMPLEX YARN & TEXTURE YARN

COMPLEX YARN

MERCERIZED YARN

Treated with mercerization to enhance its luster or to improve the strength of the yarn.

METALLIC YARN

Extruded metallic strip or continuous-filament yarn with deposited metal, usually with a protective coating, which can be clear or colored.

ELASTIC YARN

Extensive yarn wrapped with inextensive fibers by spinning, covering or uptwisting.

COMPOSITE YARN

Composed of both staple and continuous-filament yarn.

CORE YARN

TEXTURE YARN

TEXTURE YARN

Continuous-filament yarn that goes through a production process that creates durable crimps, coils and loops.

CURLED YARN

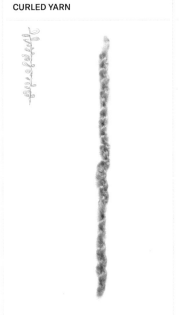

HIGH BULK YARN

LOFTED EFFECT YARN

STRETCH CORE YARN

‾WEAVES

Weaving is one of the oldest and most popular methods of textile production.

Weaving is a fabric construction method that interlaces two or more sets of yarn to form a two-dimensional woven fabric. The fiber, yarn, and weaving structure used will affect the characteristics of a woven fabric.

01

PLAIN / TABBY / TAFFETA / LINEN / PANAMA

A simple interlacing method which is found in half of woven fabrics. The warp thread is interlaced over the weft thread by alternately lifting and lowering the yarn. The result is a strong, firm fabric.

02

RIBBED / POPLIN / UNBALANCED PLAIN

A variation of plain weave, often woven with two weft-threads and one warp-thread, or weft or warp yarns, of different weights. The weft yarn is often thicker or doubled in this weave, resulting in a prominent ribbing texture that travels along the fabric horizontally.

03

BASKET / HOPSACK / CELTIC

A variation of plain weave, woven with more than one thread. Two or more warp yarns interlace over two or more weft threads, resulting in a matt weave which has flexibility and a looser construction. It is not as durable as plain weave, and easily shrinks in the wash.

04

TWILL

One or more warp fibers alternately woven over and under one or more weft fibers repeatedly. Twill uses weft fibers as weft-faced and more warp fibers as warp-faced. This results in clear diagonal lines on the surface of the fabric, as well as a smooth front and rough back. Twill weave fabrics are often heavier, wrinkle-resistant, and more durable than plain weave.

TYPES OF TWILL

Left-hand twill / S twill Lines run from the weave's upper left to lower right	**Right-hand twill / Z twill** Lines run from the weave's upper right to lower left	**Broken twill** Combination of S and Z-twisted twill

05

SATIN

Satin is a variation of twill weave with fewer intersections of warp and weft threads. Weft yarns float over warp yarns, which results in a smooth and shiny surface. However, it makes the fabric easier to snag.

06

LENO / GAUZE

Leno uses warp yarn that is not parallel like other weaves. The adjacent warp fibers are twisted around weft fibers to form a spiral pair. The result is a strong open-weave fabric.

07

PILE

Pile is woven with ground yarns and additional yarn in loop form, which can either be cut or uncut piles, resulting in soft, absorbent, and insulating fabrics. The piles can be on one side or both sides of the fabric.

08

JACQUARD

Jacquard can be one or multiple colors and can be used to create simple or complex patterns. The back side of jacquard is the mirror image of the pattern on the front. It is often durable but with a luxurious appearance.

09

DOBBY

Dobby is a patterned, plain weave with small geometric patterns. Special dobby machines are needed to produce dobby weave. The machine selectively raises some warp threads and selectively depresses others with the help of a dobby card, resulting in a woven fabric that is comparatively flat and fine.

(3.2) THREAD COUNT

WHAT IS A THREAD COUNT?

Thread is a tightly twisted strand of two or more yarns. A thread count is the number of threads per square inch or square centimeter in a fabric.

Calculating thread count:

When a fabric has 108 warps per inch and 56 wefts per inch, the thread count is

108 + 56 = 164.

WHY IS IT IMPORTANT?

The thread count of a fabric directly affects the quality of the material. Larger fibers in a diameter take up more space, whereas a smaller thread takes up less space. Fabrics with higher thread counts are often thinner, softer and more likely to last longer.

A standard thread count can start from 100, while maximum standard can go up to 200. Any thread counts over 140 will be thin and smooth to the touch.

COMMON CHARACTERISTICS

LOW THREAD COUNT

Wider Thread Diameter (Yarn Count)
- Rough   • Stiff   • Durable

AND / OR

Loosely Woven
- Bulky   • Soft   • Fuzzy

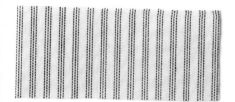

HIGH THREAD COUNT

Finer Thread Diameter (Yarn Count)
- Smooth   • Drapey   • Fragile

AND / OR

Tightly Woven
- Smooth   • Shiny   • Durable   • Crisp

(3.3) FABRIC GRAIN

Grains of woven fabrics can greatly affect the drape of a garment. Straight grain is not usually elastic, whereas true bias can be very elastic. The center fronts of the garment pieces are usually parallel to the straight grain when cut.

Lengthwise Grain / Warp
Straight of Grain

Crosswise Grain / Weft or Filling
Folded when placed on bolts

True Bias / 45° angle from the selvage

Selvage Edge — the finished edge of the fabric

(3.4) WEAVING MACHINE

There are two main types of weaving machines: shuttle looms and shuttleless looms.

SHUTTLE LOOMS

The oldest type of weaving loom, also called a fly shuttle. It can move either by hand or automatically. It provides more flexibility and works well for experimenting and sampling.

SHUTTLELESS LOOMS

Shuttleless looms are modern and run automatically. There are three main types of shuttleless looms: projectile, rapier (single or double), and water jet or air jet. All have higher productivity and are common in the industry.

1. Rapier Loom uses a rapier to pull the weft yarn across the loom.

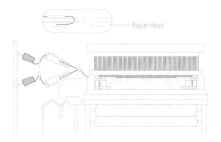

2. Projectile Loom uses a series of small bullet-like projectiles to grip the weft yarn, carry it through the shed, and return empty.

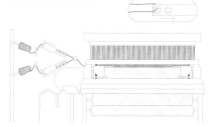

3. Jet Loom takes the weft yarn across the loom by using high-speed air or water. It has the highest productivity among all shuttleless looms.
- **Air jet** cannot be used for loosely twisted yarn.
- **Water jet** cannot be used for shrinkable yarn; it is more suitable for hydrophobic yarns.

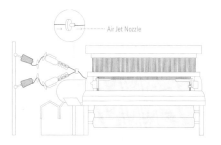

4. Jacquard Loom is an advanced version of the shuttleless loom, where each individual warp yarn is controlled by a computer to interlace with the weft yarns. It is possible to weave any graphical pattern without pattern size limitations.

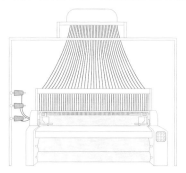

CHIFFON (LIGHT)

A sheer, slightly rough fabric often used to make elegant eveningwear.

PROPERTIES

- Slightly rough texture due to the tightly twisted crepe yarn fabrication
- Transparent due to mesh-like construction
- Drapes with a graceful flow due to being lightweight and having a loose weaving structure
- Prone to shrink and stretch due to twisted yarn fabrication
- Prone to fraying, distortion and pulled yarns due to low-density fabrication
- Difficult to handle due to its slippery texture

COMMON APPLICATIONS

Blouses

Scarves

Lingerie

Gowns

Bridalwear

Embroidery

FABRICATION

Plain weave with tightly spun S-twisted and Z-twisted crepe yarn

COMMON FIBERS

Silk, Cotton, Nylon, Polyester

VARIATIONS

CRINKLE CHIFFON: A lightweight chiffon with a subtly rough, wrinkled texture.

SATIN CHIFFON: A smooth chiffon with a satin finish on one side.

COMPARISON

WITH CREPON

P.081

	CHIFFON	CREPON
Transparency	Transparent	Semi-transparent
Thickness	Thinner	Thicker
Yarns	Highly twisted S and Z yarns	Alternating two highly twisted S and Z yarns
Texture	Coarser	Smoother

ALTERNATIVE
Georgette P.079, Organza P.082

GEORGETTE (LIGHT)

Similar to chiffon, but heavier. This durable fabric has a matte, grainy surface and is often used to make Indian saris.

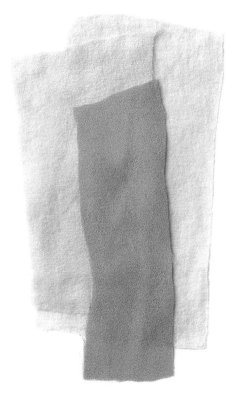

PROPERTIES

- Matte and wrinkled surface due to the alternate twist direction of the thread
- Durable and tear resistant due to its weaving structure
- Holds embroidery well due to its high tensile strength
- Prone to shrink due to crepe yarn fabrication
- Prone to pull yarns
- Difficult to handle due to the fabric's slippery edges

COMMON APPLICATIONS

Blouses   Dresses   Gowns   Saris

Lining   Scarves

FABRICATION

Plain weave alternates two tightly-spun S-twisted and Z-twisted threads in both warp and weft

COMMON FIBERS

Silk, Rayon, Polyester

VARIATIONS

JACQUARD GEORGETTE: Woven on a jacquard loom

EMBROIDERED GEORGETTE: Embellished with sequins, beadwork, or threads

SATIN GEORGETTE: Woven in satin weave and more substantial in weight

(ALTERNATIVE)

Chiffon P.078, Silk Crepe de Chine P.080, Silk Charmeuse P.110

CREPE DE CHINE (LIGHT /MEDIUM)

A crinkle-textured fabric with a slight sheen that is popular for making elegant eveningwear.

PROPERTIES

- Subtly crinkled texture and dry to the touch due to twisted yarns
- Slightly lustrous after the degumming process
- Durable and wrinkle resistant due to twisted yarns
- Clingy and static due to being a poor conductor of electricity
- Difficult to handle due to its slippery texture

STORY

Crepe de Chine means "Crepe from China" in French. The privileged Chinese imperial family favored the material during the Middle Ages. It is also common for mourning dresses and religious habits in Britain. During the 1960s, the fabric was often used to make red-carpet gowns in Hollywood.

1919 Pajamas

COMMON APPLICATIONS

Blouses

Scarves

Lingerie

Dresses

Lining

FABRICATION

Ribbed weave with 2- to 6-ply tightly spun S-twisted and Z-twisted filament yarn on weft and untwisted warp yarn

COMMON FIBERS

Silk, Rayon, Acetate, Polyester, Rayon Blend

(ALTERNATIVE)
Silk P.040, Silk Charmeuse P.110

CREPON (LIGHT)

A lightweight, pleat-like fabric that is crinkled running lengthwise, and heavier than crepe fabric.

PROPERTIES

- Semi-matte appearance, resembling crepe fabric
- Slightly transparent due to loose weave
- Not easy to crease due to its coarse pleat-like crinkle texture
- Pleat-like texture can be removed by ironing or pressing
- Difficult to handle due to its crinkled and slippery texture

COMMON APPLICATIONS

Dresses   Blouses   Suits   Home Decor

FABRICATION

Plain weave alternating tightly spun S-twisted and Z-twisted yarns

COMMON FIBERS

Cotton, Flax, Rayon, Wool, Silk

COMPARISONS

WITH SATIN CREPE AND CREPE DE CHINE

	CREPON	CREPE DE CHINE P.080
Structure	Plain weave	Ribbed weave
Texture	Pleated crinkle	Crinkled
Lustrous	Semi-matte	Matte

	SATIN CREPE P.111
Structure	Satin weave
Texture	Smooth in front, crepe at back
Lustrous	Sheen

(ALTERNATIVE)
Chiffon P.078, Georgette P.029

ORGANZA (LIGHT)

A supportive, sheer,
lightweight fabric often
used for bridal dresses.

PROPERTIES

- Stiff and crisp
- Higher-density organza is softer and smoother
- Sheer and shiny due to the combination of yarn
- Strong and durable due to its highly twisted yarn
- Prone to wrinkle and streak
- Breakage may occur along folds and creases
- Difficult to handle due to its slippery texture

COMMON APPLICATIONS

Gowns

Bridalwear

Lingerie

Veils

Gift Bags

Curtains

Home Decor

FABRICATION

Plain weave spun with tightly twisted filament yarns

VARIATIONS

ORGANDY: A cotton version of organza that is highly moldable.

COMMON FIBERS

Silk, Nylon, Rayon, Polyblend

(ALTERNATIVE)
Chiffon P.078

BATISTE (LIGHT)

A smooth, featherweight opaque fabric often used for bedding.

PROPERTIES

- Soft and smooth due to its plain weave structure
- Lightweight but durable due to its weaving structure
- Suitable for smocking and embroidery
- Drapes with a graceful flow due to being lightweight
- Does not use acid during production, making it suitable for sensitive skin

STORY

Batiste was originally a white cloth called Cambric – named after Cambrai in France, where the fabric originated. In the 13th century it was renamed as "batiste" after its inventor, Jean-Baptiste Cambray.

COMMON APPLICATIONS

| Summer Clothing | Baby Clothes | Handkerchiefs | Lingerie |

| Dresses | Linings | Curtains | Bedding |

FABRICATION

Balanced plain weave or satin weave

COMMON FIBERS

Cotton, Flax, Wool, Silk, Rayon, Poly Cotton

(ALTERNATIVE)
Voile P.084, Lawn P.085

VOILE (LIGHT)
A soft, sheer fabric often used to make lightweight curtains.

PROPERTIES

- Soft due to its high thread count
- Slightly lustrous and stiff due to the twisted yarns
- Holds a garment's shape easily due to its crisp and wiry texture
- Slightly slippery due to its tightly woven structure

STORY

French for "veil", the fabric Voile originated in the late 19th century. Primarily intended to make veils, it was initially woven from only pure cotton threads and was always white in color.

COMMON APPLICATIONS

Lingerie

Summer Clothing

Children's Clothes

Linings

Mosquito Netting

Pillowcases

Curtains

FABRICATION

Plain weave with twisted long-filament yarn

COMMON FIBERS

Cotton, Flax, Polyester, Poly Cotton, Cotton/Flax Blend

(ALTERNATIVE)
Chiffon P.078, Organza P.082, Batiste P.083, Lawn P.085, Muslin P.125

LAWN (LIGHT)

A silky, smooth, and high-thread-count fabric that is lighter than poplin.

PROPERTIES

- Soft and crisp due to its high thread count
- Crisper than voile but less crisp than organza
- Sheer but durable due to its weaving structure
- Usually finished with starch to increase crispness

STORY

Originating in the Middle Ages, the fabric lawn was named after the French city Laon, which once produced the material in large quantities.

COMMON APPLICATIONS

Dresses

Blouses

Shirts

Underwear

Lingerie

Pajamas

Handkerchiefs

Baby Clothes

FABRICATION

Plain weave with combed or carded threads

COMMON FIBERS

Flax, Cotton, Poly Cotton

COMPARISONS

WITH VOILE & BATISTE		P.083
	LAWN	BATISTE
Yarn	Combed or carded thread	Combed or carded thread
Transparency	Opaque	Semi-transparent
Drapery	Moderate	Moderate

	P.084	
	VOILE	
Yarn	Twisted threads	
Transparency	Transparent	
Drapery	Drape	

POPLIN (LIGHT / MEDIUM)

A tightly woven, finely ribbed broadcloth-like fabric often used for shirting.

PROPERTIES

- Soft due to its weaving structure
- Durable due to its high density
- Reversible due to its weaving structure

COMMON APPLICATIONS

Dresses   Shirts   Trousers   Sportswear

Pajamas   Seatcovers

FABRICATION

Ribbed weave fabric with fine warp yarn and heavy worsted weft yarn

VARIATION

END-ON-END: Lightweight, subtly heathered textured woven fabric, also known as fil-à-fil.

COMMON FIBERS

Wool, Cotton, Silk, Rayon, Polyester, Poly Cotton

COMPARISON

WITH BROADCLOTH

	POPLIN	BROADCLOTH
Texture	Smooth	Coarse
Yarn	Thinner	Thicker

(ALTERNATIVE)
Broadcloth P.087, Chambray P.088, Oxford Cloth P.090

BROADCLOTH

(LIGHT / MEDIUM)

A lightweight, unfinished fabric that is mostly a solid color, and often mixed with poplin.

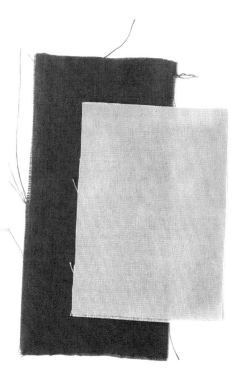

PROPERTIES

- Smooth and sturdy due to tight weave
- Slightly lustrous
- Originally woven wider than required, but shrinks afterwards
- Sheer and lightweight, especially when light colored
- Non-stretchable due to the weaving structure
- Abrades easily due to ribbed surface

STORY

Traditionally made from wool, broadcloth originated in Flanders, Belgium, during the 11th century. After the 1400s, Leiden, Holland, was home to the largest production of broadcloth, but England overtook Holland as the No. 1 producer in the 1500s. Since the 1920s, broadcloth has often been used to describe poplin fabric.

COMMON APPLICATIONS

Shirts

Dresses

Skirts

Children's Clothes

Pajamas

Bedding

FABRICATION

Ribbed weave with two twisted yarns

VARIATION

SILK FUJI: Silk-made version of broadcloth

COMMON FIBERS

Cotton, Wool, Silk, Poly Cotton

(ALTERNATIVE)
Poplin P.086

CHAMBRAY

(LIGHT / MEDIUM / HEAVY)

A lightweight plain-weave fabric that looks similar to denim, and is often used to make shirts.

PROPERTIES

- Smooth and soft due to its tight weave
- Lightweight and breathable, making it ideal for summer
- Slightly faded in appearance due to having a multicolored yarn arrangement

COMMON APPLICATIONS

Shirts

Children's Clothes

Dresses

Shorts

Sportswear

Suits

Curtains

Pillowcases

FABRICATION

Plain weave with colored warp yarn and white or unbleached weft yarn

COMMON FIBERS

Cotton, Flax, Silk, Cotton-Flax Blend, Polyblend

COMPARISON

WITH DENIM

P.092

	CHAMBRAY	DENIM
Structure	Plain weave	Twill weave
Backside of Fabric	Same appearance as front	More muted color than front
Surface	Smoother	Coarser

(ALTERNATIVE)
Oxford Cloth P.090, Denim P.092

SEERSUCKER

(LIGHT / MEDIUM)

A breathable puckered
fabric that is ideal for
making summer garments.

PROPERTIES

- Alternates between smooth and wrinkled puckered stripes or checkered patterns
- Durable due to the weaving structure
- Breathable due to the weaving structure
- Hard to tear due to its high density
- Unable to hold pleats due to puckered surface

STORY

The name seersucker was inspired by the Persian name for milk and sugar, which the smooth and rough stripes of the fabric resemble. The first seersucker fabric was made from wide, puckered white stripes of silk and cotton, and the wrinkled texture only formed after washing. In the 1940s, nurses and hospital volunteers in the United States wore outfits made of seersucker in white and red stripes, also known as "candy stripes".

COMMON APPLICATIONS

Suits

Shorts

Dresses

Shirts

Sportswear

Pillowcases

Curtains

FABRICATION

Slack tension weave

COMMON FIBERS

Cotton, Rayon, Polyester, Poly Cotton

OXFORD CLOTH (MEDIUM / HEAVY)

A casual, textured shirt fabric popular among those attending prestigious universities.

(ALTERNATIVE)

Chambray P.088, Denim P.092

PROPERTIES

- Thin checkerboard pattern due to the weaving structure
- Durable and high abrasion resistance due to its highly twisted yarn
- Generally thicker than an average shirt fabric
- Wrinkle resistant
- Easily frayed
- Slippery at the seam

STORY

Oxford Shirt

Oxford cloth was originally created in the 19th century as a marketing strategy, along with three other weaves, by a Scottish clothes maker. Each fabric was named after a famous university: Yale, Harvard, Cambridge, and Oxford. Oxford is the only university that caught on, adopting it as sportswear for polo players in the early 1900s. Today, the fabric has evolved into a staple seen in many smart casual wardrobes.

COMMON APPLICATIONS

Shirts

Sportswear

Bedding

Wall Hangings

VARIATION

PINPOINT OXFORD: A thinner and more formal version of Oxford fabric.

ROYAL OXFORD: Thinner, silkier and more luxurious than Oxford fabric, often used for formal shirting.

FABRICATION

Unbalanced 2x1 or 3x1 basket weave with highly twisted heavy yarn and white-colored weft yarn

COMMON FIBER

Cotton, Polyester, Rayon

DENIM (MEDIUM / HEAVY)

A popular and casual indigo-dyed
fabric most commonly used to
make jeans.

PROPERTIES

- Coarse texture due to its diagonal surface
- Colored warp yarn on the front, with white weft yarn on the back
- Sturdy and durable due to its weaving structure
- Softens with washing and wearing
- Holds a garment's shape well due to its stiffness
- Prone to fraying at the folded edges

STORY

Cowboy style

Denim originated during the gold rush in 1873 as a workwear fabric. The word originates from the French word "serge de Nimes", meaning "a sturdy fabric from Nimes". The United States was once the primary manufacturer of denim, but it reduced the production of high-end selvedge denim. The country's last major mill closed in 2017. Japanese denim is now widely considered to be the best quality.

COMMON APPLICATIONS

Denim Jackets

Denim Shirts

Jeans

Dungarees

Skirts

Sneakers

Bags

Seat Covers

VARIATION

RAW DENIM: Stiff with a deep blue color which is unwashed and without shrinkage.

SELVEDGE DENIM: A more premium denim, whereby the selvedges are specially woven with one- or two-color warp yarns. Garment panels can be cut to include these colored warp yarns to produce specific design effects.

COLOR-DYED DENIM: Black dyed or undyed fabric cannot officially be called denim; only indigo dyed can officially be called denim.

FABRICATION

Twill weave

COMMON FIBER

Cotton, Poly Cotton

CHINO / DRILL

(LIGHT / MEDIUM / HEAVY)

An earth-tone fabric with a diagonal brushed or mercerized surface that is widely used for trousers and sometimes called khaki.

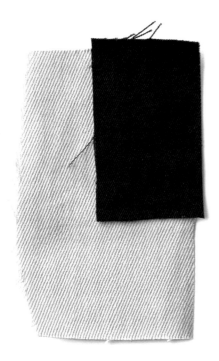

PROPERTIES

- Smooth and soft due to its brushed or mercerized surface
- Durable and abrasion resistant due to its weaving structure

STORY

Originally used for military purposes, chino grew in popularity after World War II. The fabric originated in China and was known as "pantalones chinos", Spanish for Chinese pants. The name was later simplified to chino.

COMMON APPLICATIONS

Trousers

Workwear

Suits

Bags

Uniforms

FABRICATION

Twill weave with combed yarn

COMMON FIBERS

Cotton, Poly Cotton

COMPARISON

WITH GABARDINE & CAVALRY TWILL

P.095

	CHINO	CAVALRY TWILL
Texture	Brushed or mercerized cord without specific degree	63° or 45° angle parallel cord

P.096

	GABARDINE
Texture	63° angle cord

(ALTERNATIVE)
Denim P.092, Cavalry Twill P.095, Gabardine P.096

CAVALRY TWILL

(MEDIUM / HEAVY)

A right-hand twilled fabric with parallel double ribbed lines, often used for riding breeches.

PROPERTIES

- Smooth and soft surface due to its firmly woven structure
- 63° angle raised on its surface
- Sturdy and durable due to its weaving structure
- Holds a garment's shape well, making it useful for exaggerated forms
- Prone to snagging on raised ribs

STORY

Originally cavalry twill was designed for military riding breeches, hence its association with British cavalry officers.

British cavalry officer

COMMON APPLICATIONS

Hard-Wearing Trousers

Dresses

Coats

Raincoats

Skirts

Suits

Uniforms

Bedding

FABRICATION

Twill weave

COMMON FIBERS

Wool, Worsted Wool, Cotton, Rayon, Polyblend

(ALTERNATIVE)
Denim P.092, Chino P.094, Gabardine P.086

GABARDINE (MEDIUM / HEAVY)

A durable, smooth fabric best suited for outerwear; also used to make Burberry's iconic trench coat.

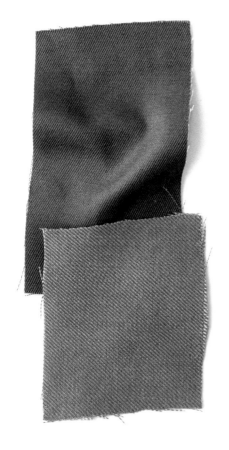

PROPERTIES

- Dull sheen finish
- 63° or 45° angle raised on its surface
- Raised lower left to upper right diagonal rib on its surface
- Durable and firm fabric due to its weaving structure
- Water resistant and windbreaking due to its tight weave
- Shine develops with wear

STORY

Burberry trench coat

Thomas Burberry adopted the name "gabardine" for the new material he had invented, and patented the name in 1888. The term was later used in reference to any raincoat or smock. The first man to reach the South Pole, Roald Amundsen, wore a Burberry jacket made of the fabric.

COMMON APPLICATIONS

Coats

Suits

Trousers

Skirts

Aprons

Workwear

Raincoats

Uniforms

FABRICATION

2x1 or 2x2 twill weave with a warp-faced steep twill

COMMON FIBERS

Cotton, Worsted Wool, Polyester, Rayon, Silk, Poly Cotton, Poly Wool

(ALTERNATIVE)
Chino P.094, Cavalry Twill P.095

SERGE (MEDIUM / HEAVY)

A double-sided, ribbed fabric often used to make military uniforms.

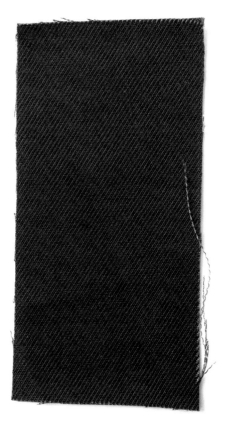

PROPERTIES

- Textured surface due to a lower left to upper right diagonal rib
- Sturdy and durable due to its weaving structure
- Wrinkle resistant, making it suitable for tailoring
- Shine develops with wear

STORY

Uniform of Royal Canadian Mounted Police

Serge is derived from the Greek word "serikos" meaning "silken". While silk serge dates back to the 8th century, wool was first used to manufacture serge in France during the 1550s; it was only available to the upper class and for military use.

COMMON APPLICATIONS

Uniforms

Suits

Coats

Jackets

Blazers

Lining

FABRICATION

Twill weave with combed yarn

COMMON FIBERS

Wool, Silk/Wool Blend, Other Blended Fibers

(ALTERNATIVE)
Denim P.092, Gabardine P.096

HERRINGBONE

(MEDIUM / HEAVY)

A distinctive fabric featuring a V-shape pattern, commonly used as suiting fabric.

PROPERTIES

- Subtle or pronounced reserved broken twill pattern
- Durable due to the firmly woven structure
- Wrinkle resistant due to its weaving structure

STORY

Herringbone is named after the skeleton of the herring, whose bones resemble the fabric's zigzag pattern. The pattern is also

Herringbone pattern resembling fishbone

known to make roads more stable and durable. Sometimes referred to as "HBT" during World War II, the fabric was often used for military purposes and was also a popular choice for suits during the 1940s.

COMMON APPLICATIONS

Coats   Suits   Skirts

FABRICATION

Twill weave with 4x4, 6x6, 8x8 or 12x12 structure thread

COMMON FIBERS

Wool, Cotton

(ALTERNATIVE)
Tweed P.116

HOPSACK (LIGHT / MEDIUM)

A subtly colored fabric that is loosely woven and suitable for summer suiting.

PROPERTIES

- Rough in texture due to its loosely woven structure
- Wrinkle resistant due to its weaving structure
- Shine develops with wear
- Prone to pull yarns due to being loosely woven

STORY

First made from jute or hemp, hopsack fabric was originally used for bagging hops, with the term being coined in England during the 19th century. Resembling basketwork, it is sometimes referred to as basket weave.

COMMON APPLICATIONS

Jackets   Trousers   Bags

FABRICATION

Basket weave

COMMON FIBERS

Cotton, Wool, Jute, Hemp, Wool/Cotton Blend

FLANNEL (LIGHT / MEDIUM / HEAVY)

A napped winter fabric used for casual shirts, commonly woven with a striped or chequered pattern.

PROPERTIES

- Soft and fuzzy due to the napped surface
- Retains heat due to its napped surface
- Prone to pilling
- Abrades easily due to the napped surface

STORY

Flannel originated in Wales in the 17th century as a replacement for plain wool outerwear. Production of flannel increased after the industrial revolution due to the invention of a mechanical carding process. Flannel became a symbol of rugged men after it was worn by soldiers and workers during the American Civil War.

COMMON APPLICATIONS

Work Shirts   Skirts   Trousers   Pajamas

Underwear   Bedding

FABRICATION

Plain or Twill weave

VARIATION

FLANNELETTE: A one-sided brushed cotton fabric imitating wool flannel.

COMMON FIBERS

Wool, Cotton, Synthetic Fiber

(ALTERNATIVE)
Velvet P.112

OTTOMAN (MEDIUM / HEAVY)

A pronounced ribbed fabric, commonly used for Queen's Counsel court gowns or academic hoods.

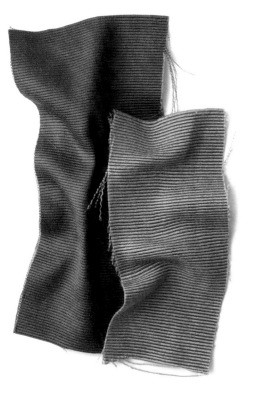

PROPERTIES

- Pronounced flat ribs in the filling direction with heavier filler yarns
- Slightly shiny
- Holds a garment's shape easily due to its stiff texture
- Retains heat due to the napped surface
- Sheds dust easily due to ribbed texture
- Unstable, tending to slip at the seams and crack
- Hard to handle due to its ribbed surface

STORY

Originating in Turkey, ottoman fabric was traditionally made using only natural silk fibers and was used for covering footstools, such as ottomans, and other furniture.

COMMON APPLICATIONS

Heavy-duty Outerwear · Suits · Dresses · Gowns

Curtains · Ribbons

FABRICATION

Basket or ribbed weave with alternating thin and heavy yarn

VARIATION

OTTOMAN CORD (OR OTTOMAN RIB): An ottoman fabric when a warp rib is used

OTTOMAN SOLEIL: An ottoman fabric consistently of narrow ribs only

COMMON FIBERS

Warp: Silk, Rayon, Acetate

Weft: Cotton, Wool, Cotton/Wool Blend

ALTERNATIVE

Bengaline P.102, Faille P.103

BENGALINE (MEDIUM)

A thick-grained fabric with raised crosswise ribs, also known as *"grosgrain"*.

PROPERTIES

- Coarse and stiff due to its corded surface and heavier weft yarn
- Durable due to its weaving structure
- Tends to fray at edges

STORY

During the 17th century, bengaline was used as the core material for many garments including jackets, waistcoats, and sleeves. In the 19th century, the fabric became a popular alternative to silk.

COMMON APPLICATIONS

Skirts	Dresses	Trousers	Jackets

Coats	Shirts	Curtains	Ribbons

FABRICATION

Ribbed weave with a fine warp and heavy weft yarn

COMMON FIBERS

Cotton, Wool, Silk, Rayon, Nylon

(ALTERNATIVE)
Ottoman P.101, Faille P.103

FAILLE (MEDIUM)

A crosswise ribbed fabric, widely used for formalwear during the 1940s and 1950s.

PROPERTIES

- Slightly stiff and crisp due to its ribbed surface
- Shiny appearance with ribs on the surface
- Sturdy due to its weaving structure
- Wrinkle and tear resistant due to its stiff texture

COMMON APPLICATIONS

Dresses

Coats

Blouses

Suits

Skirts

Scarves

Curtains

Gowns

FABRICATION

Ribbed weave

COMMON FIBERS

Cotton, Silk, Wool, Rayon, Acetate

COMPARISON

COMPARISON WITH BENGALINE & OTTOMAN

P.102

	FAILLE	BENGALINE
Texture	Fine ribs	Raised crosswise rib

P.101

	OTTOMAN
Texture	Largest and rounded ribs

ALTERNATIVE
Ottoman P.101, Bengaline P.102

MIKADO (MEDIUM / HEAVY)

A stiff fabric with a slight sheen, commonly used for winter wedding dresses.

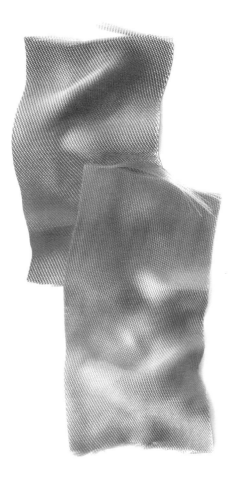

PROPERTIES

- Stiff due to its subtle texture
- Slightly shiny due to its silk fiber
- Durable due to its weaving structure
- Holds a garment's shape well, making it ideal for exaggerated silhouettes

COMMON APPLICATIONS

Gowns   Dresses   Blouses   Trousers

Coats   Blazers   Skirts

FABRICATION

Twill weave

COMMON FIBERS

Silk, Polyester

(ALTERNATIVE)
Satin P.108

TAFFETA (MEDIUM)

A stiff fabric that rustles when rubbed; some comes with an iridescent multicolored sheen.

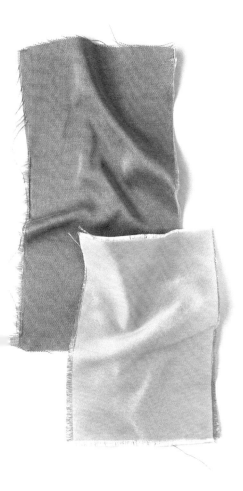

PROPERTIES

- Crisp and smooth
- Shiny; often has a multicolored iridescent sheen due to the different colored yarns
- Makes a rustling sound with movement due to the fabric's crispness
- Hold a garment's shape well due to stiff texture
- Hard to handle due to a slippery surface

STORY

Originating from the Persian word "taffeta" meaning "twisted woven", taffeta was used in an aviation experiment in the 18th century by Joseph Montgolfier. Lightweight synthetic forms of taffeta are used to simulate blood vessels in experiments.

Princess Diana's wedding dress

APPLICATION

Gowns	Jackets	Sportswear	Lingerie
Suits	Dresses	Sleeping Bags	Handbags

FABRICATION

Ribbed weave

COMMON FIBERS

Silk, Nylon, Acetate, Polyester, Rayon, Polyester, Nylon Blends

(ALTERNATIVE)
Shantung P.107, Dupioni P.106

DUPIONI (LIGHT / MEDIUM)
A lightweight, iridescent silk fabric with rough thread reels on the surface.

PROPERTIES

- Crisp and stiff due to its raw fiber
- Rough texture with occasional small slubs on the weft
- Iridescent appearance due to the multicolored threads
- Holds a garment's shape well due to its stiff texture
- Prone to unravel at the edges

STORY

The name dupioni comes from the Italian word for double, "doppio". The name is a reference to the uneven weft threads made by worms in two or more cocoons.

COMMON APPLICATIONS

Jackets   Blouses   Skirts   Bridalwear

Home Decor   Table Runners

FABRICATION

Plain weave with uneven weft thread reels and different colored warp threads

COMMON FIBERS

Silk

(ALTERNATIVE)
Taffeta P.105, Shantung P.107

SHANTUNG (LIGHT / MEDIUM)

The heaviest type of silk fabric, lighter than dupioni, it is often used for bridal gowns.

PROPERTIES

- Stiff and crisp texture due to the weaving structure
- Regular slubs due to the uneven thickness of the warp
- Subtle iridescent effect when woven with multicolored warp and weft yarn
- Lustrous on surface
- Holds a garment's shape well due to its stiff texture
- Difficult to handle due to slubs

STORY

The name shantung is derived from the province of Shandong, China, where the fabric originated.

COMMON APPLICATIONS

Gowns   Bridalwear   Suits

FABRICATION

Ribbed weave

COMMON FIBERS

Cotton, Silk, Polyester

(ALTERNATIVE)
Taffeta P.105, Dupioni P.106

SATIN (LIGHT / MEDIUM)
A glossy, luxury fabric often used for nightgowns.

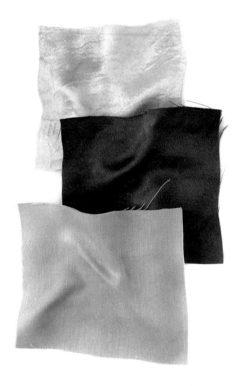

PROPERTIES

- Smooth and lustrous due to the weaving structure
- Silky appearance on the front of the fabric, dull on the back
- Prone to snagging and breakage due to its smooth surface
- Difficult to handle due to its slippery texture

STORY

Until the 1800s, satin was commonly used in dressmaking – most often to make evening gowns for upper and working-class women to wear only once. King Louis XIV of France was also known to cover his ornate furniture in the Palace of Versailles with the luxurious fabric during the 1600s and 1700s.

Satin dress

COMMON APPLICATIONS

Gowns

Dresses

Corsets

Lingerie

Baseball Jackets

Shirts

Ties

Bedding

FABRICATION

Satin weave with floating warp yarn

VARIATION

SATEEN: Satin weaved with combed or carded long cotton fiber, widely used in elegant apparel.

COMMON FIBERS

Silk, Wool, Nylon, Polyester, Silk/Cotton Blend

(ALTERNATIVE)
Duchess Satin P.109, Charmeuse P.110,
Satin Crepe P.111

DUCHESS SATIN

(MEDIUM / HEAVY)

A high-thread-count satin fabric, suitable for embroidery and mainly used for bridal dresses.

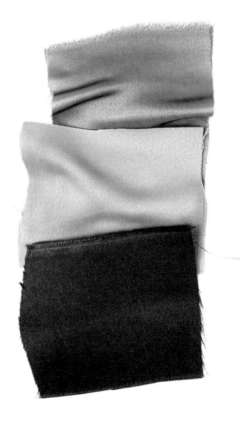

PROPERTIES

- Stiff and heavy due to the tightly woven structure
- Shiny on the surface due to the weaving structure
- Holds a garment's shape well due to its stiff texture
- Prone to fraying at the edges

COMMON APPLICATIONS

| Embroidery | Gowns | Bridalwear |

FABRICATION

Satin weave

COMMON FIBERS

Silk, Polyester, Rayon, Acetate, Silk Blend

(ALTERNATIVE)
Satin P.108, Charmeuse P.110

CHARMEUSE

(LIGHT / MEDIUM)

A lightweight, shiny, thin satin-like fabric, popular for lingerie and evening gowns, which was once called *"the fabric of the emperors"*.

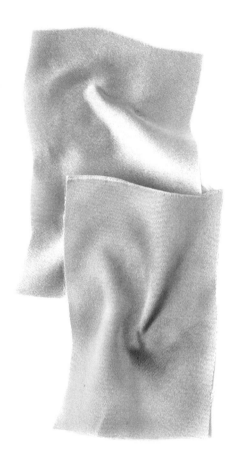

PROPERTIES

- Very lustrous in the front, very dull at back
- Slightly reflective due to the weaving structure
- Soft; drapes with a graceful flow
- Prone to snagging due to its smooth surface
- Difficult to handle due to its slippery surface

STORY

The origin of the word charmeuse comes from the French word meaning "charming female". Traditionally, charmeuse was associated with the nobility.

Charmeuse sleepwear

COMMON APPLICATIONS

| Gowns | Blouses | Lingerie | Skirts |

| Shorts | Ties | Bedding | Handkerchiefs |

FABRICATION

Satin weave with 4 or more floating warp threads

COMMON FIBERS

Silk, Polyester, Rayon

(ALTERNATIVE)

Satin P.108, Duchess Satin P.109, Satin Crepe P.111

SATIN CREPE (MEDIUM)

A reversible satin fabric,
sometimes called
"crepe-back satin".

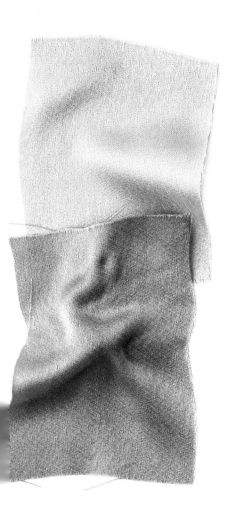

PROPERTIES

- Slightly silky appearance on the front with crepe texture at the back, due to the weaving of the yarns
- Flowing drape due to its weaving structure
- Prone to snagging and stretching due to its smooth and delicate surface

COMMON APPLICATIONS

Gowns   Skirts   Blouses   Trousers

Scarves   Linings

FABRICATION

Satin weave with highly twisted yarn on the weft and low-twist yarn on the warp

COMMON FIBERS

Silk, Polyester

(ALTERNATIVE)
Satin P.108, Charmeuse P.110

VELVET (MEDIUM / HEAVY)

A luxurious, glossy winter fabric
with silken short nap.

(ALTERNATIVE)

Flannel P.100, Corduroy P.114

PROPERTIES

- Soft and smooth surface due to its short nap
- Direction of nap influences the glossiness of the fabric
- Easily frayed due to the nap
- Crushed or matted nap appears in patches and can look like stains
- Difficult to handle and maintain due to the napped surface

STORY

Due to velvet's higher price and luxurious appearance, it has long been a symbol of prestige and power, and is often associated with royalty. Renaissance velvet, which incorporates silk and precious metal threads, was used to make clothing for kings, queens, and members of the church during the medieval period. King Richard II of England was said to have asked for his body be draped in velvet after he died. In the 1960s, villains in Hindi movies frequently wore velvet jackets.

Princess Diana's Travolta dress

COMMON APPLICATIONS

Gowns

Blazers

Trousers

Suits

Gloves

Curtains

FABRICATION

Pile weave

COMMON FIBERS

Silk, Cotton, Flax, Wool, Rayon, Polyester, Nylon, Acetate, Silk/Rayon Blend

VARIATION

VELVETEEN
A cotton version of velvet that has less sheen and is usually slightly stretchable.

VELOUR
A knitted version of velvet that has a V-back knit.

COMPARISON

	WITH VELVETEEN & CORDUROY	
	VELVET	VELVETEEN
Pile Length	Slightly longer	Shorter (no more than 3mm)
Surface	Sheen	Less Sheen

	CORDUROY
Pile Length	Similar to velveteen
Surface	Corded surface sheen

CORDUROY (MEDIUM / HEAVY)

A heavyweight winter fabric with a soft corded nap on its surface, commonly used for urban workers' uniforms.

PROPERTIES

- Smooth and soft due to its cut-pile brushed nap
- Twill-weave backs are more durable
- Durable due to its weaving structure
- Naps tend to shed on a plain-weave back
- Naps tend to mat with pressure or abrasion
- Brushed or matted pile appears in spots and can look like a stain

STORY

Corduroy was first woven from silk to create clothes for the nobility during the 18th century.

During the industrial revolution in England, corduroy started to be created from cotton and became a working-class fabric. It also became a popular choice for upholstering cars.

Corduroy workwear jacket

After the Beatles helped popularize corduroy again in the 1960s, it became associated with British country clothing.

COMMON APPLICATIONS

Trousers   Jackets   Work Shirts   Cushions

Dungarees   Soft Toys

FABRICATION

Cut pile weave

COMMON FIBERS

Cotton, Wool, Silk, Polyester, Rayon, Cotton/Spandex Blend

WALE NUMBER

Wales measure the width of the cord by counting the number of ridges per inch.

6-WALE: JUMBO — Trousers

8-WALE: WIDE — Trousers

11-WALE: STANDARD — Jacket, Shirt, Dress, Trousers

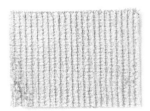

16-WALE: PINWALE — Jacket, Shirt, Dress, Trousers

21+ WALE: FEATHER — Shirt, Dress

TWEED (MEDIUM / HEAVY)

A durable fabric commonly used for outdoor clothing, as well as Chanel's iconic suit jackets.

PROPERTIES

- Durable; tightly woven with multi-ply yarn
- Easily hides stitches due to its rough surface
- Retains heat, able to keep warmth
- Wrinkle resistant
- Tends to stretch with time

STORY

Tweed originated in Scotland and Ireland as a fabric used for farmers' clothing. First known as "tweel", the Scottish for "twill", the name tweed came into use around 1831 after a London merchant misinterpreted the handwriting in a letter. The fabric became synonymous with British hunting-inspired clothing in the 19th century. Coco Chanel also

famously reworked tweed fabric with a more loosely woven design into suit jackets, which remain one of the most iconic pieces of fashion. In the UK, in 1993, an Act of Parliament was passed

The Chanel look of the early 1960s

to maintain the authenticity, standard, and reputation of Harris Tweed – the most famous tweed.

COMMON APPLICATIONS

| Jackets | Coats | Gloves | Trousers |

FABRICATION

Plain weave / Twill weave

TYPES OF TWEED

Tweed can be named after the type of wool, its geographical origin, the manufacturer, or the function of the cloth. Well-known types of tweed are Harris, Donegal, and Saxony.

COMMON FIBERS

Wool, Wool/Cotton Blend, Silk, Rayon, Viscose

COMMON PATTERNS OF TWEED FABRIC

OVERCHECK

OVERCHECK HERRINGBONE

HERRINGBONE

BARLEYCORN

STRIPED

HOUNDSTOOTH

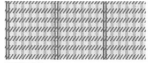

CHECKED

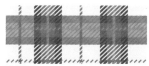

TARTAN

PLAID TWILL TWEED

DAMASK (MEDIUM / HEAVY)

A decoratively woven jacquard fabric that is usually monochromatic.

PROPERTIES

- Flat, reversible pattern on its surface
- Durable due to its high density
- Prone to fraying or pulling due to its raised woven pattern

STORY

Originally made of cotton and silk, damask is named after Damascus – the capital of the Syrian Arab Republic and the place where explorer Marco Polo replenished his supplies. Damask was introduced to Europe in the 11th century by crusaders.

COMMON APPLICATIONS

Curtains · Tablecloths · Bedding

FABRICATION

Jacquard weave

COMMON FIBERS

Silk, Satin, Wool, Cotton, Polyester, Rayon

(ALTERNATIVE)
Brocade P.119

BROCADE (MEDIUM / HEAVY)

A more luxurious version of jacquard, woven on twill or satin and often weaved with metallic threads.

FRONT

BACK

PROPERTIES

- Rich and lustrous with an intricate pattern on one side
- Prone to fraying or pulling due to its woven pattern
- Difficult to handle due to its irregular surface

STORY

Brocade was first woven on looms from silk in 1766 BC. Europeans started weaving brocade, which was worn by emperors and the very wealthy, in the 15th century. The fabric was usually encrusted with jewels and hand-embroidered to make clothes and tapestries.

COMMON APPLICATIONS

| Gowns | Blazers | Coats | Suits |

| Dresses | Robes | Tablecloths | Bedding |

FABRICATION

Jacquard weave with extra weft threads

COMMON FIBERS

Cotton, Silk

REMARK

	DAMASK	BROCADE
Back	Reversible, same color as the front	Irreversible, reversed, or contrasting color with the front
Pattern	Similar color with fabric ground	Usually made with metallic or contrasting colored yarn

(ALTERNATIVE)
Damask P.118

TERRY CLOTH

(MEDIUM / HEAVY)

A popular toweling fabric with highly absorbent loops on its surface.

PROPERTIES

- Soft uncut loops on its surface
- Retains heat and warmth due to its looped surface
- Able to absorb water over 20 to 30 times its weight due to the loops
- Loops tend to mat and change texture with pressure or abrasion

STORY

The first terry cloth was made of silk and produced in 1841. By the mid-19th century, England had begun mass-producing cotton terry cloth.

Chanel tracksuit, spring/summer 1996

COMMON APPLICATIONS

Sweatshirts

Towels

Loungewear

Cloth Diapers

Pillowcases

Embroidery

Soft Toys

FABRICATION

Pile weave

COMMON FIBERS

Cotton, Silk, Bamboo, Cashmere, Polyester, Nylon, Poly Cotton

REMARK

French terry cloth is a warp knitted fabric similar to standard terry cloth.

(ALTERNATIVE)
Microfiber P.054

SAILCLOTH

(LIGHT / MEDIUM / HEAVY)

A fabric often used
for sails.

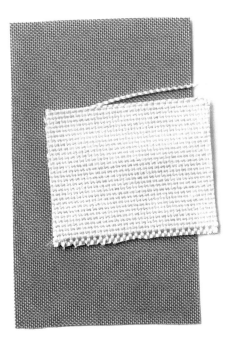

PROPERTIES

- Smooth and frictionless due to the interlocked flattened fibers
- Durable and stretchable due to being loosely woven
- Absorbs shock well due to its weaving structure

STORY

Originally made from linen, in the 19th century, sailcloth switched to cotton due to the large quantities available in the United States. In the late 20th century, sailcloth made from synthetic fiber grew in popularity.

COMMON APPLICATIONS

Sportswear

Bags

Cushions

Curtains

Sails

Tents

FABRICATION

Balanced or unbalanced basket weave

COMMON FIBERS

Flax, Hemp, Cotton, Nylon, Polyester

(ALTERNATIVE)
Canvas / Duck P.122

CANVAS (LIGHT / MEDIUM)

A heavy-duty fabric commonly used as a surface for paintings, with two variations: plain and duck.

(ALTERNATIVE)

Denim P.092, Sailcloth P.121, Calico P.124, Buckram P.127

PROPERTIES

- Stiff with a coarse texture
- Rugged surface with cross-grain ribbing
- Durable due to its weaving structure
- Stress and tugging resistant

STORY

The name canvas is derived from the Latin and Greek word "cannapaceus", meaning "made of hemp".

Converse signature Chuck Taylor shoes

APPLICATION

| Jackets | Jeans | Backpacks | Sneakers |
| Sails | Tents | Painting Surface | |

FABRICATION

Basket weave

COMMON FIBERS

Cotton, Hemp, Poly Cotton

VARIATION

DUCK: A basket-weave cotton fabric with two warp yarns and a single weft yarn. It is coarser and heavier than canvas.

DUCK CLASSIFICATION		
№ 1	18oz.	Hammocks, cots, sandbags
№ 2	17oz.	Hatch tarpaulins
№ 3	16oz.	Heavy-duty bags
№ 4	15oz.	Sea bags
№ 5	14oz.	Heavy workwear
№ 6	13oz.	Large boat covers, heavy work clothes
№ 8	11oz.	Work clothes, clothes bags
№ 10	9oz.	Work clothes, shower curtains
№ 12	7oz.	Light clothes

CALICO (LIGHT / MEDIUM / HEAVY)

An undyed fabric with visible flecks of cotton seeds, mainly used for mock-up garments.

PROPERTIES

- Unfinished, natural look due to its coarse and slightly fuzzy surface
- Durable due to its weaving structure
- Softens with washing
- Holds a garment's shape well due to texture's stiffness
- Heavyweight calico is difficult to quilt due to its rigidity

STORY

First mentioned in Indian literature during the 12th century, calico was originally called "calicut". Originating in the Indian city of Calicut, it was the first Indian plain-weave cotton. However, the import of dyed or printed calico was later banned in Europe, while the demand for unfinished calico increased.

Practice fabric

COMMON APPLICATIONS

Aprons   Curtains   Pillowcases

Tote Bags   Practice Fabric

FABRICATION

Plain weave

COMMON FIBERS

Half-Processed Unbleached Cotton, Poly Cotton

(ALTERNATIVE)
Canvas P.122, Muslin P.125

MUSLIN (LIGHT / MEDIUM)

A loosely woven fabric, most commonly used for test garments.

PROPERTIES

- Slightly crisp and stiff due to identical warp and weft yarn
- Semi-transparent and breathable due to a loose plain weave
- Soft but durable
- Tends to stretch with wear
- Prone to wrinkle and shrink

STORY

First produced in Mosul, Iraq – hence the name – muslin has been around since ancient times. Handwoven with extremely fine hand-spun yarn, the fabric was a popular choice for clothing in France during the Regency era of the 1800s.

Muslin towels

COMMON APPLICATIONS

Baby clothes   Quilts   Curtains   Practice Fabric

FABRICATION

Balanced plain weave

COMMON FIBERS

Cotton, Silk, Wool

(ALTERNATIVE)
Canvas P.122, Calico P.124

BURLAP (LIGHT / MEDIUM / HEAVY)

A coarse fabric commonly used to make storage sacks, also called Hessian.

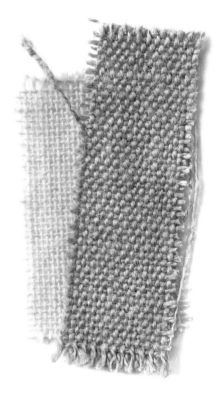

PROPERTIES

- Coarse and scratchy texture due to raw natural plant fiber
- Durable due to the high strength and weaving structure
- Tear resistant
- Prone to shedding fibers due to raw threads
- Slubs on fabric can become crooked during stitching and break the needle
- Biodegradable due to the natural fibers

COMMON APPLICATIONS

Storage Bags   Home Decor   Rope

FABRICATION

Plain weave

COMMON FIBERS

Jute, Hemp, Flax

BUCKRAM

(LIGHT / MEDIUM / HEAVY)

A stiff, supportive fabric soaked with resin and starch, mainly used for interfacing.

PROPERTIES

- Coarse due to its small, rough, hair-covered surface
- Stiff due to fabric finishing and loose weave
- Durable due to the fabric finishing
- Non-permanent fabric finishing, which is easily removed when cleaned
- Easily molded to shapes when wet
- Shrink and tear resistant

COMMON APPLICATIONS

Garment Interfacing | Costume Shaping | Millinery Stiffening | Bookbinding

FABRICATION

Plain weave

COMMON FIBERS

Cotton, Jute, Hemp

GAUZE (LIGHT / MEDIUM)

A translucent fabric
commonly used for
surgical dressings.

PROPERTIES

- Coarse surface but soft to the touch
- Open-mesh surface
- Stable and slip-proof due to its interlocking warp and weft yarn
- Sheer and breathable due to its loosely woven structure
- Easily unravels and is prone to curling at the edges

COMMON APPLICATIONS

Blouses

Shirts

Dresses

Skirts

Blankets

Baby
Clothes

Surgical
Dressings

FABRICATION

Balanced plain weave with interweaving pairs
of warp yarn looped on weft

COMMON FIBERS

Silk, Wool, Rayon

(ALTERNATIVE)
Voile P.084, Marquisette P.129

MARQUISETTE

(MEDIUM)

A sheer, gauze-like mesh fabric, often used for mosquito nets.

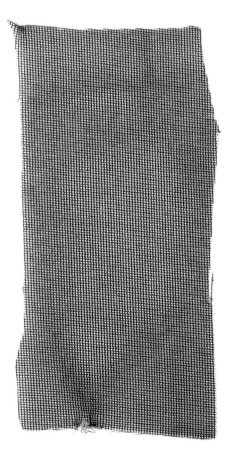

PROPERTIES

- Texture can be soft, crisp, or coarse depending on the material used
- Stiff enough to be used for structural design
- Breathable due to its open weave
- Wrinkle resistant due to its weaving structure

STORY

Originally made from silk, marquisette was a popular decorative fabric for evening and bridal gowns in the 19th century. Today it is more commonly used for net curtains.

COMMON APPLICATIONS

Gowns

Bridalwear

Curtains

Mosquito Netting

Millinery

FABRICATION

Leno weave

COMMON FIBERS

Silk, Cotton, Wool, Rayon, Nylon, Polyester, Blended fibers

(ALTERNATIVE)
Gauze P.128

(3.5) COMPARISON

SUITS

	GABARDINE	HERRINGBONE	TWEED	HOPSACK	BENGALINE
	P.096	P.098	P.116	P.099	P.102
CONSTRUCTION	Twill weave 2X1/ 2X2	Twill weave 4X4 / 8X8 / 12X12	Twill weave	Basket weave	Ribbed weave with fine warp and heavy weft yarn
COMMON FIBERS	Worsted Wool, Cotton, Silk	Wool, Cotton	Wool, Wool/Cotton Blend/Silk/Rayon, Textured yarn	Cotton, Wool, Jute, Hemp, Wool/Cotton Blend	Cotton, Wool, Silk, Rayon, Nylon
SHININESS	Matte	Matte	Matte	Matte	Sheen
SOFTNESS	Crisp	Soft	Soft but tough	Soft	Crisp

CASUAL SHIRTS

	CHAMBRAY	OXFORD CLOTH	DENIM	FLANNEL	SEERSUCKER
	P.088	P.090	P.092	P.100	P.089
CONSTRUCTION	Plain weave with colored warp and white or unbleached weft yarn	Unbalanced basket weave with high twist warp and thick weft yarn	Twill weave 2X1/ 3X1	Plain weave	Slack tension weave with bunched threads
COMMON FIBERS	Cotton, Cotton/Flax Blend	Cotton, Polyester, Rayon	Cotton, PolyCotton	Wool, Cotton, Synthetic	Cotton, Rayon, Polyester
SHININESS	Matte / faded look	Matte	Matte	Matte	Matte
HAND FEEL	Smooth	Slightly coarse	Coarse	Smooth	Slightly coarse
SOFTNESS	Soft	Crisp	Stiff	Soft *Napped surface	Crisp

DRESS SHIRTS

	BROADCLOTH	PINPOINT OXFORD	ROYAL OXFORD	HERRINGBONE	BATISTE	POPLIN
	P.087	P.090	P.083	P.086		

CONSTRUCTION						
	Ribbed weave with two twisted threads	Basket weave with light and fine weft and warp threads	Dobby weave 2X1	Twill weave 4X4/ 6X6 / 8X8	Plain weave	Ribbed weave

COMMON FIBERS						
	Cotton, PolyCotton	Cotton, Polyester, Rayon	Cotton, Polyester, Rayon	Wool, Cotton	Cotton, Wool, Silk, Rayon, Linen	Wool, Cotton, Silk, Rayon, Polyester

SHININESS						
	Matte	Matte	Matte	Matte	Sheen	Shiny

HAND FEEL						
	Smooth	Smooth	Smooth	Coarse	Smooth	Smooth

SOFTNESS						
	Soft	Soft	Soft	Soft	Crisp	Crisp

DRAPEY						
	—	—	—	—	—	—

REMARKS						
	Fine, less texture	Fine basket-weave texture	Diamond structure on surface	2:1 45° rotated rectangle pattern	—	—

WORKWEAR

P.092	P.122	P.095	P.094	P.097	P.114
DENIM	**CANVAS/ DUCK**	**CAVALRY TWILL**	**CHINO**	**SERGE**	**CORDUROY**

CONSTRUCTION

Twill weave 2X1/ 2X2	Pile weave with double piece loom	Twill weave	Ribbed weave	Jacquard weave with extra weft threads	Jacquard weave

COMMON FIBERS

Cotton, Cotton blend with polyester	Cotton, Hemp, Flax	Wool, Cotton, Rayon	Cotton, PolyCotton	Wool, Silk	Cotton, Wool, Silk, Cotton/ Spandex Blend, Polyester, Rayon

SHININESS

Matte	Matte	Matte	Matte	Shiny	Matte

HAND FEEL

Coarse	Coarse	Coarse	Smooth	Smooth	Smooth

SOFTNESS

Stiff	Crisp	Soft	Crisp	Crisp	Soft

DRAPEY

—	—	—	—	—	—

REMARKS

—	—	63° parallel rib on surface	Diagonal brushed surface	Diagonal rib from lower left to upper right	Brushed cut pile nap surface

COATS

	GABARDINE	VELVET	CANVAS/ DUCK	FAILLE	BROCADE	DAMASK
	P.102	P.112	P.122	P.103	P.119	P.118
CONSTRUCTION	Twill weave 2X1/ 2X2	Pile weave with double piece loom	Basket weave	Ribbed weave	Jacquard weave with extra weft threads	Jacquard weave
COMMON FIBERS	Worsted Wool, Cotton, Silk	Silk, Wool, Cotton, Flax, Rayon, Polyester, Nylon, Acetate	Cotton, Hemp, Flax	Cotton, Silk, Rayon, Acetate	Silk, Cotton	Silk, Wool, Linen, Cotton, Polyester, Rayon
SHININESS	Shiny	Shiny	Matte	Shiny	Shiny	Shiny
HAND FEEL	Smooth	Smooth	Coarse	Smooth	Smooth	Smooth
SOFTNESS	Crisp	Soft	Crisp	Crisp	Soft	Soft
DRAPEY	Moderate drape	Full-bodied drape	Moderate drape	Full-bodied drape	Moderate drape	Moderate drape
REMARKS	45° or 63° angle rib on surface	<0.36cm height of nap	—	Ribbed surface	Pattern only shows on one side	Reversible pattern at fabric back

[3.2] COMPARISON

TEXTURED EVENINGWEAR

	CHIFFON	SATIN CREPE	GEORGETTE	CREPE DE CHINE	DUPIONI	CREPON
	P.078	P.111	P.079	P.080	P.106	P.081
CONSTRUCTION	Plain weave with highly twisted yarn	Satin weave with low-twist warp and high-twist weft	Plain weave with high-twist S and Z threads	Plain weave with crepe Z-twisted filling	Plain weave with uneven thread reels	Plain weave with high-twist S and Z yarns
COMMON FIBERS	Silk, Cotton, Nylon, Polyester	Silk, Polyester	Silk, Rayon, Polyester	Silk, Rayon, Acetate, Polyester/Rayon Blend	Silk	Silk, Cotton, Linen, Rayon
SHININESS	Shiny	Shiny	Matte	Matte	Shiny	Matte
HAND FEEL	Coarse	Smooth	Coarse	Coarse	Coarse	Coarse
SOFTNESS	Stiff	Crisp	Soft	Crisp	Crisp	Soft
DRAPEY	Fluid drape	Crisp drape	Crisp drape	Full-bodied drape	Moderate drape	Fluid drape
REMARKS	—	Crepe texture on back	Crinkle surface	—	Small slubs at warp	Pleat-like crinkle effect

SMOOTH EVENINGWEAR

	ORGANZA	SATIN	TAFFETA	CHARMEUSE	DUCHESS SATIN	MIKADO
CONSTRUCTION	Plain weave with highly twisted yarn	Satin weave	Ribbed weave	Satin weave	Satin weave with long floats yarn	Twill weave
FIBERS	Silk, Nylon, Rayon, Polyester	Silk, Nylon, Polyester, Wool, Silk/Cotton Blend	Silk, Nylon, Acetate	Silk, Polyester, Rayon	Silk, Polyester, Rayon, Acetate	Silk, Polyester
SHININESS	Shiny	Shiny	Shiny	Shiny	Shiny	Matte
HAND FEEL	Silky, slippery	Smooth	Smooth	Smooth	Smooth	Smooth
SOFTNESS	Crisp	Silky	Crisp	Silky	Crisp	Soft
DRAPEY	Moderate drape	Full-bodied drape	Moderate drape	Fluid drape	Moderate drape	Moderate drape
REMARKS	—	—	Sometimes with multiple colors on surface	Slightly reflective	Dull back	—

KNITS

Knitting is forming a series of courses and multiple loops of yarn to create a textile.

There are two main types of knitting: warp knitting and weft knitting, each of which can be created by hand or machine. There are many variations of knitting structures and patterns that have evolved from basic knitting principles. Different types of yarn, stitches, and gauge contribute to different characteristics.

(4.1) TYPES OF KNIT

Depending on the direction of the threads, knitted fabric can be divided into two main types: weft or warp.

HAND KNITTING	MACHINE KNITTING

 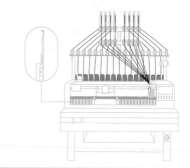

WEFT KNITTING	WARP KNITTING

Weft knitting refers to flat and circular weft knitted fabrics. In weft knitting, which is more commonly used, the loops are formed running horizontally across the width of the fabric.

Warp knitted fabrics are produced using different technologies to weft knitting. The loops are formed running vertically in a zigzag manner along the length of the fabric. This allows for more complicated designs and textiles to be created. It is less common than weft knitting.

Circular Weft Knitted Fabric   Flat Weft Knitted Fabric

Warp Knitted Fabric

(4.2) WALES & COURSES

WALES: Vertical columns of stitches and vertical chains of loops in the lengthwise direction of the fabric.

COURSES: Horizontal rows of stitches that run widthwise, along with rows of loops or stitches running across the knitted fabric.

KNITTING DIRECTION: In weft knitting, the entire fabric is usually produced from a single yarn, with the wales and courses running roughly perpendicular. In warp knitting, the wales and courses run roughly parallel.

 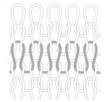

Weft Knitted Fabric: Wale   Weft Knitted Fabric: Course

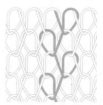 

Warp Knitted Fabric: Wale   Warp Knitted Fabric: Course

4.3 TYPES OF STITCHES

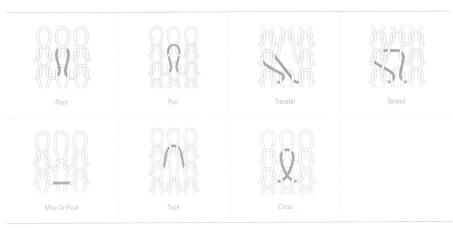

| Plain | Purl | Transfer | Spread |

| Mise Or Float | Tuck | Cross |

4.4 MACHINE GAUGE AND CHOICE OF YARN COUNT

Machine gauge refers to the gauge of knitting machine from which a fabric is made, and shows how many needles are present in one inch of fabric. It can be applied to both warp and weft knitted fabric.

(Higher the machine gauge number) = (Closer the needles) = (Finer the knit)

	GAUGE NUMBER	APPLICATION
COARSE GAUGE	1.5 / 3 / 5 / 7 / 9 / 10 / 12	Sweater, knitwear
FINE GAUGE	14 / 16 / 18	
	20-30	Smooth menswear T-shirts
	30-40	Fine womenswear T-shirts

STITCH TENSION

Stitch tension is used to determine if the fabric is knitted adequately (not too tight or too loose). Slack fabric requires fewer wales and less yarn.

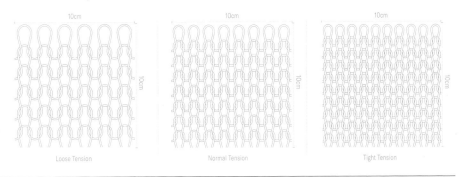

| Loose Tension | Normal Tension | Tight Tension |

(4.3) CUTTING OF KNITTED FABRIC

Cutting knitted fabric can be done in three ways:

ALL CUT

All garment pieces are cut from fabric, then sewn together

ADVANTAGES

- Higher production rate
- Low-cost fabric without progressive narrowing

DISADVANTAGES

- Labor intensive
- Higher fabric waste

Fold

Collars

FULLY FASHIONED

Pieces of the garment are knitted into the exact shape required, then joined using a dial-linking machine

ADVANTAGES

- Little or no cutting waste
- Effective production

DISADVANTAGES

- Lower volume of production

Cut

Collars

INTEGRAL

Garments are produced as one piece. Sometimes the end and beginning of the garments are joined

ADVANTAGES

- Low labour cost
- Low wastage
- Saves sewing time

DISADVANTAGES

- A more experienced technician is needed to operate the machine

Cut

Collars

(4.4) KNITTING MACHINES

There are three main types of knitting machine: a flat-bed, a circular-bed for weft knitting, and a warp knitting machine.

FLAT BED

There are single bed and double bed (V-bed) machines available in both hand or machine versions. They are used to produce pieces of clothing or whole garments, usually with thicker yarn. Seamless garments are produced by programmed flat-bed machines.

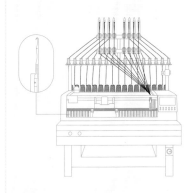

CIRCULAR BED

Circular-bed knitting machines create tube-shaped pieces and are often used for larger and faster production. They are also commonly used to produce finer knitwear.

	FLAT BED KNITTING MACHINE	CIRCULAR KNITTING MACHINE
COMMON GAUGE	1.5-18	Over 20
TEXTURE	Less fine than circular knitting	Finer and thinner than flat bed knitting
GARMENT PRODUCT	All methods applicable	Only supports all cut

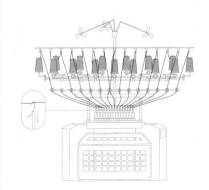

WARP MACHINE

Warp knitting machines are divided into two types: Tricot and Raschel. Tricot machines usually handle finer knitting and are used to produce garments such as sportswear and intimates. Raschel machines handle coarser knits, producing lace and other technical textiles.

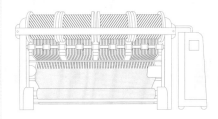

JERSEY / PLAIN KNIT

Jersey, also called single knit, or stockinette, is one of the most basic forms of weft knitting. The back side is known as reverse knit.

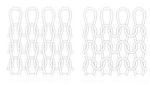

Produced on machines with one set of needles.

FRONT — V-shaped stitches

BACK — Interlacing semicircular loops

COMMON APPLICATIONS

T-shirts

Underwear

Sportswear

Baby Clothes

CHARACTERISTICS

- Irreversible knit
- Smooth technical front and rough technical back
- Lightweight in comparison with other knits
- Yarn can be pulled out from both the first course and the last course
- Curls toward the front at both ends and toward the back along the sides

KNITTING DIAGRAM

1

2

DOUBLE JERSEY
Double jersey, also known as double rib, full-needle rib, and 1x1 all-needle rib.

Produced on machines with two sets of needles.

FRONT — A single wale of face loops alternates with a single wale of back loops

BACK — A single wale of face loops alternates with a single wale of back loops

COMMON APPLICATIONS

Polo Shirts

Underwear

Sportswear

Sweaters

CHARACTERISTICS

- Reversible knit
- Double thickness and weight of 1x1 rib fabric
- More stable and compact
- Has equal tension on each side and does not curl at the edges
- Only ladders* from the end of the fabric that was last knitted

*A ladder forms when a stitch is broken. A wale will disintegrate and slip through the previous loop, causing a ladder in the material.

KNITTING DIAGRAM

1
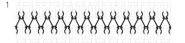

2
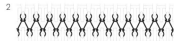

RIB KNIT

Rib knit is a double-faced knit with distinct vertical columns on both sides. It can be formed by various numbers of plain and purl stitch ridges.

Produced by two sets of needles with the opposite needles offset. The heads of the needles are not facing each other directly.

SAME NUMBER OF PLAIN AND PURL RIDGES (REVERSIBLE)

1X1 RIB / PLAIN RIB

Every other wale alternates between plain and purl stitches on the right and back sides.

FRONT (TOP) & BACK (BOTTOM) — A single wales of face loops alternates with a single wale of back loops.

2X2 RIB / SWISS RIB

Every two wales of plain stitches on the front side alternate with every two wales of purl stitches on the back side.

FRONT (TOP) & BACK (BOTTOM) — 2 adjacent wales of face loops alternate with 2 adjacent wales of back loops in series.

1X1 RIB KNITTING DIAGRAM

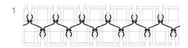

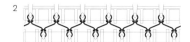

2X2 RIB KNITTING DIAGRAM

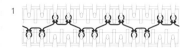

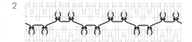

DIFFERENT NUMBER OF PLAIN AND PURL RIDGES (IRREVERSIBLE)

2X1 RIB

Every two wales of plain stitches on the front side alternate with one wale of purl stitches on the back side.

FRONT (TOP) & BACK (BOTTOM) — 2 adjacent wales of face loops alternate with 1 adjacent wale of back loops in series.

COMMON APPLICATIONS

1x1 Rib / 2x2 Rib / 2x1 Rib

Ribs with a high number of consecutive rib wales

Cuffs

Neckbands

Complete and Body-fitted Garments

Waistbands

BROAD RIB

Structures may have different combinations of plain and purl stitch wales, such as 2x2 (Swiss rib), 6x3 (Derby rib), and 10x3.

FRONT (TOP) & BACK (BOTTOM) — 6 adjacent wales of face loops alternate with 3 adjacent wales of back loops in series.

CHARACTERISTICS

- Reversible when the number of knit and purl stripes are equal
- Durable and dense to the touch
- Excellent widthwise elasticity, and purl knit column may be hidden if very fine yarns are used
- Elasticity decreases when the number of wales in each rib increases
- The edge of rib fabric does not curl

INTERLOCK

Interlock is an alternative double bed 1x1 rib jersey, but with a faint twill pattern.

2 courses of loops show that the wales of face loops on each side of the fabric are opposite to each other, thus hiding the appearance of the purl loops

FRONT — Same appearance and smooth surface on both sides

BACK — Same appearance and smooth surface on both sides

COMMON APPLICATIONS

Jackets

Tanks / Camisoles

Sportswear

Baby Clothes

CHARACTERISTICS

- Reversible and smooth
- Different from rib fabric, the purl rows can be seen when stretched out
- Firm textures
- Does not shrink as much as the 1x1 rib fabric
- Lengthwise elasticity better than widthwise
- No tendency to roll, and does not curl at the edges
- Can be unraveled only from the end last knitted

KNITTING DIAGRAM

1

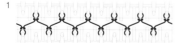

2

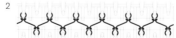

REVERSE / PURL KNIT

Purl knit, also best known for producing link or links knit, has the appearance of a plain knit back on both sides.

FRONT –

BACK –

COMMON APPLICATIONS

Polo Shirts

Underwear

Sportswear

Sweaters

CHARACTERISTICS

- Reversible
- Low density and lightweight
- Less stable than interlock knit
- Lengthwise elasticity is double of plain knit
- Does not curl
- Easy to unravel from both ends
- Not often used on its own

(4.4) COMPARISON OF 4 BASIC KNITS

	JERSEY	RIB
APPEARANCE	Different face and back (V shapes on face, arcs on back)	Same on both sides, back side of plain knit
UNRAVELLING	Either end	Only from end knitted last
CURLING	Tendency to curl	No tendency to curl
THICKNESS AND WARMTH	Thicker and warmer than woven made from same yarn	Much thicker and warmer than plain
EXTENSIBILITY (LENGTHWISE)	Moderate	Moderate
EXTENSIBILITY (WIDTHWISE)	High	Very high
EXTENSIBILITY (AREA)	Moderate to high	High
COMMON APPLICATIONS	T-shirts Fine Cardigans Dresses Sweaters	Socks Underwear Waistbands Sweaters

	INTERLOCK	PURL
APPEARANCE	Same on both sides, face of plain knit	Same on both sides, back side of plain knit
UNRAVELLING	Only from end knitted last	Either end
CURLING	No tendency to curl	No tendency to curl
THICKNESS & WARMTH	Very much thicker and warmer than plain	Very much thicker and warmer than plain
EXTENSIBILITY (LENGTHWISE)	Moderate	Very high
EXTENSIBILITY (WIDTHWISE)	Moderate	High
EXTENSIBILITY (AREA)	Moderate	Very high
COMMON APPLICATIONS	Underwear Shirts Suits Sportswear	Children's Clothes Sweaters Outerwear

HALF MILANO

Half Milano, also known as semi-double knit, is an irreversible rib-based fabric with a 2-course repeat structure.

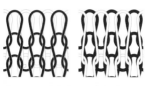

2-course repeat structure consisting of one row of plain rib and one row of plain knitting made on either set of needles.

FRONT — 1 Long held course in 1 repeat

BACK — 2 courses in 1 repeat

COMMON APPLICATIONS

Sweaters

CHARACTERISTICS

- Irreversible
- Higher stability and firmer grip than plain rib
- No rolling tendency, can stabilize edges of jersey panels
- Curling occurs toward the "single-course face"
- Only unravels from the end that was last knitted
- Ladder resistant

KNITTING DIAGRAM

1

2

FULL MILANO

Full Milano, also known as double knit, is a reversible knit with a 3-course repeat structure.

A 3-course repeat structure with 1 revolution of tubular knit after 1 plain rib course

FRONT — V-shaped stitches

BACK — Interlacing semicircular loops

COMMON APPLICATIONS

Sweaters

Skirts

Trousers

Suits

CHARACTERISTICS

- Reversible
- Stiff and high density
- Does not curl at the edges due to the balanced fabric loop tension
- Only unravels from the end that was last knitted
- Ladder resistant

KNITTING DIAGRAM

1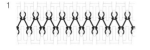

2

3

HALF CARDIGAN

Half cardigan, also called royal rib, is a modified form of tucked rib knit fabric where the face side resembles beads.

Tuck loops on one side only on alternating courses

FRONT — Even and flat

BACK — Same as both sides of full cardigan, coarser and more grained than front

COMMON APPLICATIONS

Cardigans

Baby Clothes

Sweaters

CHARACTERISTICS

- Irreversible due to unbalanced knit structure
- Closer wales on face side than full cardigan
- Smooth
- Dense and stable
- High elasticity, especially in horizontal direction
- Does not curl

KNITTING DIAGRAM

1

2

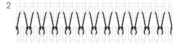

FULL CARDIGAN

Full cardigan, also known as polka rib or full tuck, is a reversible, bulky and heavy knit repeating 2-course of 1x1 rib structure.

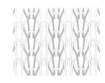

A 2-course repeat 1x1 rib. When one side is knitted, the opposite side is tucked, and vice versa in the other course.

FRONT — V-shaped stitches

BACK — Interlacing semicircular loops

COMMON APPLICATIONS

Body Sections of Heavyweight Stitch Shaped Sweaters

CHARACTERISTICS

- Reversible
- Rib wales are separated by a tuck stitch
- Tuck loops increase the fabric's thickness and make it heavier and bulkier
- High elasticity, especially in the horizontal direction
- Does not roll and curl

KNITTING DIAGRAM

1
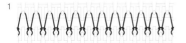

2

CABLE

Cables are wales or groups of adjacent wales that cross over another wale or group of adjacent wales, resulting in a cabled effect.

---

1. SIMPLE CABLE

FRONT

BACK

- Two-stitch cable crossed every 4th row (baby cable)
- Four-stitch cable crossed every 6th row

- Six-stitch cable crossed every 8th row (Master cable)

2. HORSESHOE CABLE

3. PLAIT CABLE

- Also called Butterfly Cable, Double Cable, Reverse double cable

4. SLIP-CROSS CABLE

5. CABLE & ARAN DIAMOND

COMMON APPLICATIONS

Sweaters

Hats

Blankets

Rugs

CHARACTERISTICS

- Thick cable knits are perfect for creating a chunky effect
- Cables can trap air to retain warmth
- Less flexibility than other knitted fabrics

JACQUARD

Jacquard describes designs that use different colored yarns. The needles making the face of the fabric are selected to knit and miss. It is the simplest method of making patterned fabrics.

There are two types of jacquard: single-jersey (also known as float jacquard or Fair Isle), and double jacquard.

Using miss stitches to create patterns on the front of a single-jersey jacquard creates floating yarns on the back of the fabric.

FRONT

BACK — The "miss" stitch causes floating yarns at the back of the fabric

COMMON APPLICATIONS

Ties   Pullovers   Cardigans

CHARACTERISTICS

- Floats are visible on the back of single-jersey jacquards
- Snagging occurs easily due to the floats

DOUBLE JACQUARD

A rib jacquard which overcomes the problem of floats in single-jersey jacquards. There are various types of rib jacquard, each named according to the type of backing, with birdseye being the most popular.

FRONT — V-shaped stitches

BACK — Interlacing semicircular loops

COMMON APPLICATIONS

Hats   Scarves   Blankets   Rugs

CHARACTERISTICS

- Reversible fabric
- Thicker than single-jersey jacquard since it is double-sided
- Lower elasticity than other knitted fabrics

INTARSIA

Derived from the Italian word for "*inlay*", intarsia is a decorative knit used for lightweight color-patterned knits.

FRONT

BACK — The "miss" stitch causes floating yarns at the back of fabric

COMMON APPLICATIONS

Socks

Scarves

Sweaters

CHARACTERISTICS

- Both sides look very much alike
- Smooth on the right side
- Lightweight
- Curled on the top and bottom edges
- Pixelated edge of colored area

TUBULAR KNIT

Tubular welt is a welt made on a rib basis. It is used to create a clear, neat edge. It is usually called French welt when knitted at the beginning, and split welt when it is knitted at the end.

Consists of an equal number of plain courses on each set of needles

APPLICATIONS

Collars and Plackets

Sleeve Cuffs

Waistbands and Hems

CHARACTERISTICS

- Reversible double-faced fabric
- High lengthwise elasticity
- Only the top of the fabric curls while the other three edges lie flat

KNITTING DIAGRAM

1

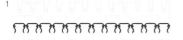

2

TRICOT

Tricot is a two-course repeated warp
knitted structure. Each column of
loops has its own threads.

Interlocked zigzag on
each column

FRONT — Rib knit pattern

BACK — Weft rib knit pattern

VARIATIONS

1. **Jersey tricot:** A stretchy tricot fabric generally
   used for lingerie

2. **Satin tricot:** A smooth, lustrous tricot fabric
   used for intimate apparel

3. **Mesh tricot:** An eyelet patterned fabric often
   used for sportswear

4. **Brushed tricot:** A brushed fabric with nap on the surface,
   commonly used for pockets or linings.

COMMON APPLICATIONS

Lingerie

Swimwear

Sportswear

Blouses

CHARACTERISTICS

- Different look on both sides
- Smooth front surface with different textured rib back
- Edges easily curl when cut
- Sturdy resistance to pulling

RASCHEL

Raschel is a warp-knitted, lace-like structure that can be used to inlay and connect yarns.

Usually starts with 28, 36 or 48 gauge. Using a finer yarn to interlock with heavy and textured yarn

FRONT — An open-construction knit that is able to create various looks.

BACK — An open construction knit which able to create various looks.

COMMON APPLICATIONS

Curtains

Blankets

Dresses

Lace Edging

CHARACTERISTICS

- Reversible or single-face with various knitting possibilities
- Low extension ability
- Does not curl at the edges
- Hard to snag or ravel
- Greater dimensions and stability than weft knit

05

LACE & NETTING

Lace and net are delicate openwork fabrics.

Lace is a patterned, openwork, delicate mesh fabric. Netting is a mesh material with open spaces. Both lace and netting can be made by hand or machine using loops, knits, or interlacing threads.

5.1 STRUCTURE OF LACE

Lace can be identified by its design or pattern. These patterns are constructed of different parts, each having a particular name.

APPLIQUÉ

A motif applied on a base fabric.

CORDONNET

A thick and heavy raised thread used to outline a lace pattern or motif. The outline can be worked on using a buttonhole stitch, chain stitch, or couching.

BRIDES / BARS / TIES / BRIDGES

Connecting threads that link the motifs and lace design. They are used to hold or connect lace without a mesh base. Connection threads can be made using buttonhole stitches, twisted threads, corded strips, or narrowed fabric.

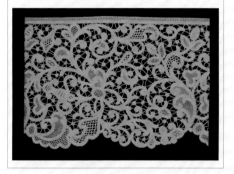

CHAIN STITCH

BUTTONHOLE STITCH

COUCHING

FILET

Using a darning stitch to fill a mesh ground or knotted net.

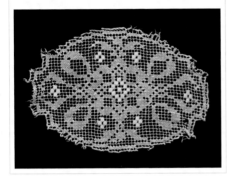

GROUND

A mesh or net background of a lace, joined with patterns. The ground can be identified as one of the three following types:

BRIDE GROUND
(grounds formed by bridges)

RÉSEAU GROUND
(net ground)

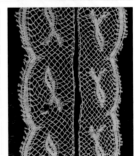

PICOT

A thread loop that forms part of the surface of the pattern or has the same function as the bride.

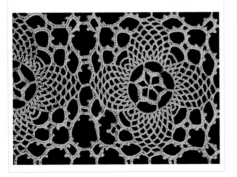

MESH
(machine net)

(5.2) HANDMADE

Handmade lace has been used throughout history to display wealth and demonstrate the good taste of the wearer. It can be expensive due to it being rare and often time-consuming to make, and requiring exquisite craftsmanship.

NEEDLEPOINT LACE	A single-thread technique used to create a buttonhole or blanket stitch.	
ALENÇON	Popular in the 18th century, Alençon – also called the "Queen of Lace" – is made using twisted stitches on a mesh base with flower patterns. Patterns are decorated on the edges with cordonnet and picots.	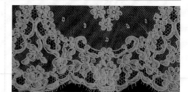
ROSE POINT (POINT DE ROSE OR POINT DE GAZE)	A mid-weight lace, finished with little loops and rosette motifs. Usually surrounded by tulle, it is commonly used for bridal veils, handkerchiefs, and collars.	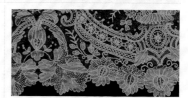
GROS POINT (POINT DE VENISE)	Gros point is a heavyweight lace produced during the 17th century. Created by packed twisted stitches, patterns are outlined with cordonnet and raised using bridges.	

EMBROIDERED & EMBROIDERED NET LACE		
	Patterns are stitched on a sheer woven fabric or tulle base. Buttonholes, overcasts, or chin stitches are applied to form the lace.	
BURATTO	Extra darning threads are applied on a square mesh, creating a pictorial pattern. Buratto tends to use heavyweight lace.	

CROCHETED LACE

A single thread forms a loop chain of stitches, which creates a lace pattern. Popular in the mid-19th century, the lace is commonly used for trimmings and collars.

FILET CROCHET

Chain stitching and double crochet stitching creates a grid-like pattern. It is usually applied on window curtains, tablecloths, and placemats.

IRISH CROCHET

Irish crochet is created by hooking mesh stitches, or using chains and picots to join motifs together, rather than being created in rounds and rows.

HAIRPIN CROCHET

This technique is used to form a lightweight lace pattern. It is created by wrapping threads around the prongs, forming a spine in the center.

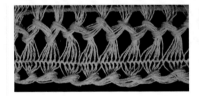

KNOTTED LACE

TATTING

A circular lace using threads to form a series of knots and loops with rings and chains. Tatting is usually applied on lace edging, accessories, or decorative pieces.

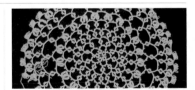

MACRAMÉ

Made from multiple threads, the lace is formed using square or reef knots through a knotting technique.

[5.2] HANDMADE

BOBBIN LACE (PILLOW LACE)	Multiple threads wind lace around a bobbin, creating grounded continuous forms and bars, or a non-continuous lace form. Sewing bars or brides link the pattern on a mesh ground.	
GUIPURE	The motifs of guipure are connected with bars or brides, rather than net or mesh, with thick outlines. During the Middle Ages, guipure was only used for the clothing of kings' or queens' servants or for the wealthy.	
BLONDE	A natural-colored or black lace made with silk. It incorporates flower motifs with thicker threads on a light point or kat stitch base ground.	
	KAT STITCH GROUND (LEFT) **POINT GROUND** (RIGHT)	
MALTESE	A cloth stitch wound, guipure-style bobbin lace featuring Maltese crosses connected by bars or brides made from cream-colored silk. Wheat motifs are commonly seen in this type of lace.	
TORCHON (BEGGAR'S LACE)	A white, coarse lace featuring simple geometric patterns and straight lines. Often used for edging, insertion, and trimming cotton or linen underwear, it was popular with the middle class in the 17th century.	
VALENCIENNES	A strong, firm, diamond-shaped patterned net lace made without cordonnet and often applied to bed linen, lingerie, and fichus.	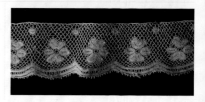

ANTWERP	A six-pointed star or hexagonal lace base featuring a repeated lily motif. Popular as trimming during the 16th century and primarily exported to Spanish American colonies.	
MECHLIN	A lightweight hexagonal base featuring floral patterns and made using loosely twisted silk cordonnet. Primarily used for decorating women's clothing.	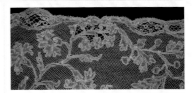
HONITON	Separately made lace joined with finely threaded motifs using bars, net, and filling stitches. Common motifs are daisies, roses, ivy leaves, acorns, and lilies.	
CHANTILLY	A thin, untwisted cordonnet outlined pattern that sits on a fine base. Light and shadow is created by half-and-whole stitches. Black Chantilly lace was popular for mourning garments during the eras of Louis XV and Louis XVI.	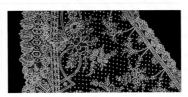
TAPE LACE	Tape lace, also known as mixed lace, is a machine-made lace that uses a needle lace filling technique to fill in the gaps of a pattern.	
RENAISSANCE LACE	A machine-made outline and tape are paired on glazed cloth or paper. A buttonhole stitch or other stitches are used to fill the gaps. The lace is then cut from the cloth or paper.	
BRANSCOMBE	This lace creates floral motifs using a light and open tape filled with tight needle lace stitches or bars. Decorated with picots, it was created by John Tucker in the late 1860s.	
BATTENBERG	Named to honor a wedding in the Battenberg family, this heavyweight lace consists of small geometric patterns that uses 8mm tape sewn with decorative stitches.	

(5.3) MACHINE MADE

Lace machines were developed to increase the speed of lace-making. Many types of lace, ranging from very fine and delicate to heavyweight, can be produced by lace machines. Most machine-made lace uses floral or geometric patterns on mesh or netted bases.

LEAVERS MACHINE

Leavers machines are able to produce versatile, lightweight lace with complex fine patterns.

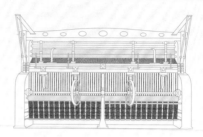

RASCHEL MACHINE

Similar to the Raschel machine used in warp knitting, this is able to produce lace similar to the Leavers machine but at a higher working speed.

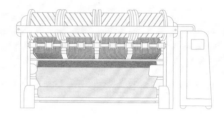

CIRCULAR LACE MACHINE

Circular lace machines echo the circular knitting machine and produce braiding lace.

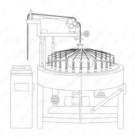

SCHIFFLI MACHINE

A Schiffli machine is often used to produce chemical, guipure, and embroidered lace. It can also be used to create three-dimensional effects.

Other machines, such as the bobbinet, are commonly used to produce heavyweight bold lace. The pusher is able to produce lace in larger amounts.

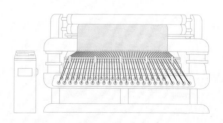

(5.4) TIMELINE While it is difficult to determine the exact origin of lace, the first mention of it is in the 15th century. Popularity grew in the 16th century and the first unravel wide-net machine lace emerged toward the end of the 18th century.

1950
NYLON AND POLYESTER
Mostly Leavers or Raschel machine made

RAYON
Mostly Leavers machine lace and is difficult to tell from silk
1915

1900
COTTON
Often used with another fiber in machine lace

SILK
Common in black lace
1700

1600
LINEN
Often used for finer lace and as outlining thread with cotton

(5.5) TYPES OF NETTING

Delicate yet durable, netting is an open-mesh material consisting of lots of spaces or holes. The holes are mainly geometric in shape and are determined by the manufacturing method. The type and size of the yarn, finishing, shape, and size of the holes determines the type and function of the netting. Nets can also be embroidered or decorated with appliqués such as sequins to enrich the material for clothing or costume construction.

COMMON NETTING

TULLE

The most famous netting fabric, tulle is lightweight, features fine nets made with finer yarns, and has small hexagonal holes. Of a low denier count and softer than other netting fabrics, it is often made of silk or nylon yarn and is best for making overskirts, ruffles, trims, and evening dresses.

BOBBINET

Bobbinet is similar to tulle, but heavier, often leading to the two being confused. A strong lace-like net with hexagonal holes, it is commonly used for bridal veils and other bridalwear to add shape and fullness to the garment. Being a sturdy and supportive base fabric, it is also used for embellished garments.

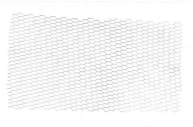

FISHNET

This is a slightly coarse netting made from knotted yarn, using knots similar to a fisherman's knot. It is often made of polyester or nylon yarn and commonly has elastane fibers for stretchiness. Fishnet is used to make hosiery, bodysuits, body stockings, and other clothing.

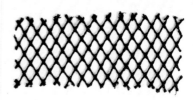

COMMON FIBERS

Nets can be made of different fibers, such as silk, polyester, rayon, acetate, or nylon, and can be fine, coarse, or stiff. A silk net can be very soft, whereas nylon netting is rather stiff. Most nets in fabric shops are usually nylon.

MILLINERY VEILING

SIMPLE NET / VEILING

The most commonly used net in millinery. Decorative veiling, pearls, or diamonds can be added as embroidery.

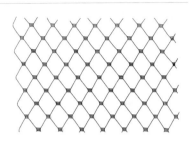

HONEYCOMB NET / VEILING

Experiencing an increased demand of late, it has a more defined appearance than simple veiling.

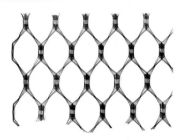

SINAMAY

A popular hat-making foundation, often woven from abaca stalks.

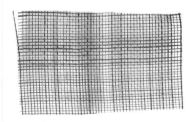

HORSEHAIR BRAID / CRINOLINE

Horsehair braid, also called crinoline netting, was originally made from horsehair. It is used to stabilize the hem and give it structure.

NON-
WOVEN
&

06

FELTING

Both non-woven and felting are fabrics formed by chemical or mechanical treatments without using a weaving or knitting process.

176
↓
183

Non-woven refers to fabrics that are neither woven or knitted. They are fabrics formed through methods that entangle and bond fibers mechanically, thermally, or chemically.

There are plenty of possibilities and outcomes when it comes to the process of creating non-woven fabrics.

(6.1) GENERAL PRODUCTION PROCESS OF NON-WOVEN

The production of non-woven fabric can be divided into web forming or bonding. Both ways determine the properties and end use of the fabric.

FIBROUS ⟶ (Web Forming) ⟶ (Bonding Process) ⟶ (Finishing)

PARALLEL LAID

Higher strength in one direction, but weaker in the other

CROSS LAID

A more even distribution of strength

RANDOM DEPOSITION

Strength in all directions

(6.2) WEB FORMATION

This process transforms fibers, filaments, films, or thermoplastic resins into layers. Fiber networks are called webs, batts, mats, or sheets.

STAPLE FIBER WEB

DRY-LAID

A mechanical process used to align combed stapled fibers and create a light form with a carding machine.

FIBER LENGTH:
17.8 - 149.9mm staple fibers / 0.76 - 7.6mm short cut pulp fibers

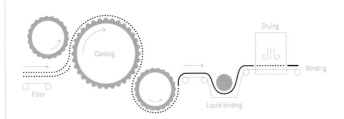

AIR-LAID

Fibers are dispersed in the air and collected on a moving belt to form a randomly oriented web. The fabric usually has a lower density but greater softness than carding.

FIBER LENGTH:
12.7 - 101.6mm staple fibers or pulp fibers

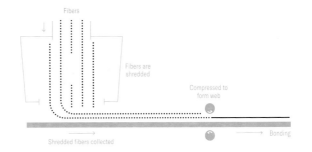

WET-LAID

Similar to paper making, the process involves a mixture of fibers in water, which are collected on a screen, drained, and then dried. It is best for large-scale productions.

FIBER LENGTH:
6.4 - 19.1mm polymer fibers or pulp fibers

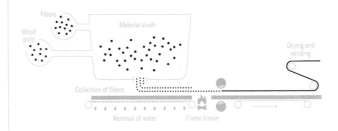

FILAMENT

SPUN-LAID

Melted polymers are extruded through many small holes and collected on a belt. The filaments adhere to each other before cooling down. Fabric will have greater strength, but lower flexibility.

FIBER LENGTH: Endless polymer filament fibers

*Spun-laid web is also self-bonded during the web forming process

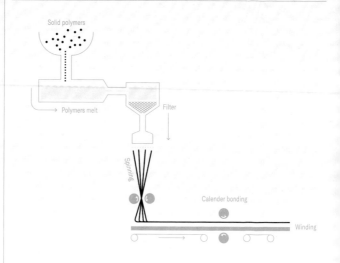

MELTBLOWN

Finer than spun-bonded fabrics, molten polymers are extruded and drawn with high-speed hot air to form a fine filament.

FIBER: Endless polymer filament fibers

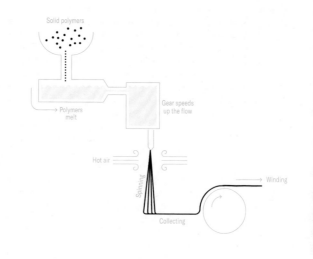

(6.3) BONDING

Holds fibers together to form a more solid non-woven fabric. Bonding determines a fabric's strength, porosity, flexibility, softness, and density. Some finishing can be added during the bonding process.

BONDING

THERMAL BONDING

Uses heat energy and pressure to bond webs. Suitable for low-melting and heat-sensitive synthetic fibers.

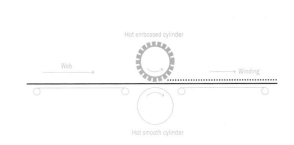

MECHANICAL BONDING

Creates friction within the fabric to entangle the fibers. There are two types of mechanical bonding:

① **Needle Punching** — used to bond dry-laid and spun-laid webs
Stitch bonding: Knits columns of stitches down the length of the web

② **Hydroentanglement/ Spunlace** — uses a high-pressure water jet to entangle the fibers

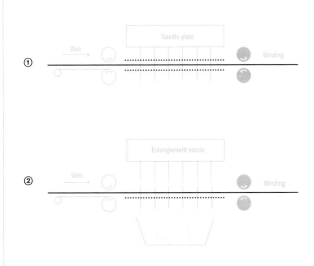

CHEMICAL BONDING

Applies a liquid-based bonding agent to form the fabric.

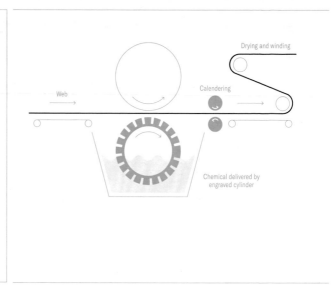

Drying and winding

Web

Calendering

Chemical delivered by engraved cylinder

(6.4) FORMATION METHOD

	DRY-LAID / AIR-LAID	WET-LAID	SPUN-LAID / MELTBLOWN
RAW MATERIAL	Staple fiber (Synthetic / Natural)	Staple fiber (Synthetic / Natural)	Filament fiber (Synthetic)
FIBER DEPOSIT DIRECTION	Parallel fibers / random deposit	Random deposit / cross laid fiber	Random deposit / cross laid fiber
	Cloth-like texture often used for clothing and sanitary products	Bamboo-like texture, often used for medical and industrial applications	
BONDING METHOD	All mechanical, thermal, and chemical bonding methods are able to bond non-woven fabric		

6.5 FELTING

Felt is a non-woven fabric considered to be the oldest known textile. The sheet-shaped fabric is produced by compressing scaled animal hair.

FELTING

WELT FELTING

The scales of fibers are opened by wetting and soaping fibers in hot water. Agitating them causes them to latch onto each other, creating felt. Only animal fibers covered in tiny scales can be wet felted; plant and synthetic fibers cannot.

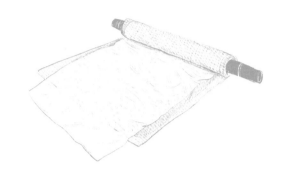

NEEDLE FELTING

Needle felt is produced without the use of water but with special "barbed" needles that have notches along the shaft. Needle felting is used in both industrial processes and individual crafting, using various sizes and types of notched needles.

(6.5) COMMON APPLICATIONS

WEB FORMATION
Mostly dry-laid

BONDING
All bonding methods
applicable

CLOTHING, FOOTWEAR, BAGGAGE

INTERLINING

Front of overcoats, collars, facings, waistbands, lapels

DISPOSABLE GARMENTS

Underwear, apron, napkins

PROTECTIVE GARMENTS

Headgear, gloves

BRAS AND SHOULDER PADS

RELEVANT PROPERTIES

- Non-raveling edge
- Easily cut, sewed, glued, and trimmed without fray
- High tear and abrasion resistance

SHOE & BAG COMPONENTS

Shoe sole linings, bag straps

COMPOSITION & LAUNDRY LABELS

SUBSTRATE FOR SYNTHETIC LEATHER & MAN-MADE SUEDE

FELTED WOOL FABRIC

07

HIDES

Leather is animal skin that can be used as a fabric.

Leather, hide, or skin is animal skin that has had the hair removed. Leather from smaller animals is called skin, whereas leather from larger animals is called hide. Animal leather normally goes through cutting and tanning treatment, with faux leather being produced from synthetic materials as an alternative to animal skin. The application of leather is decided by its thickness, grading, and source.

⑦.1 TYPES OF LEATHER

Leather can be made from the skins of different animals, all of which have unique shapes, sizes, and different qualities.

COW FULL HIDE	COW HALF HIDE	COW SHOULDER

LAMB FULL HIDE	PIG HIDE	ALLIGATOR HIDE
		PYTHON SKIN

⑦.2 BEST PART

Different parts of a hide will differ in quality, even within the same piece.

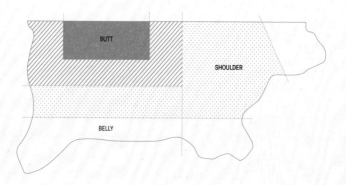

BEST
GOOD
FAIR
POOR

BUTT

SHOULDER

BELLY

(7.3) IMPERFECTIONS

Leather is a natural byproduct, and certain imperfections will exist. Common imperfections include scars, bug bites, and wrinkles. This will affect the grading and selling price.

WRINKLES

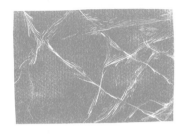

SCRATCHES

SCARS

BUG BITES

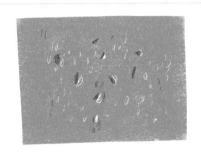

GRADING

The grading system rates the damage or defects found in leather, but does not completely reflect the quality of the piece. Even though the grade of the leather is one of the factors that affects its price, it can still be subjective and only experienced leather traders can truly determine the quality and value of the piece.

GRADE A No imperfections, marks, or scars

GRADE B 5 - 10% imperfections

GRADE C 10 - 20% imperfections

GRADE D 20 - 30% imperfections

GRADE E 30 - 40% imperfections

GRADE F Factory rejected

(7.4) CLASSIFICATIONS OF LEATHER

The layers of a hide have different impacts on quality and final use. Generally, there are four types of layers: full grain, top grain, split / genuine, and reconstituted / bonded leather.

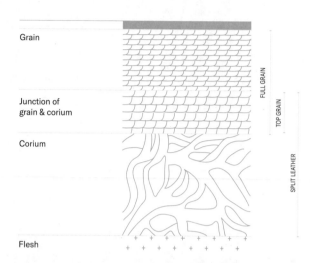

Grain

Junction of grain & corium

Corium

Flesh

FULL GRAIN

TOP GRAIN

SPLIT LEATHER

FULL GRAIN

QUALITY ★★★★

COMMON APPLICATIONS

High-quality Furniture · Luggage

Footwear

- Entire grain layer is kept, hence high strength and durability
- Shows all natural markings and grains
- No sanding and buffing needed to remove imperfections
- Develops a patina (a soft sheen) over time

TOP GRAIN

QUALITY ★★★☆

COMMON APPLICATIONS

High-end Products · Handbags

- Imperfections or thin grain surface are removed
- Thinner, since it is usually buffed and sanded
- Usually has a finishing and is smooth to touch

VARIATIONS: Corrected grain is commonly top grain embossed with artificial grain and is often used to imitate exotic leather.

SPLIT / GENUINE

QUALITY ★★☆☆

COMMON APPLICATIONS

Low-cost Furniture · Low-cost Garment

- Grain layer removed
- Thicker hide can be further divided into multiple layers
- Thinner, less durable and absorbs liquid more easily

VARIATIONS: Suede is a napped, split leather that has been sanded; bicast leather is split leather with a vinyl embossed layer applied to the surface; patent leather is split leather with a high-gloss coating and is similar to bicast.

RECONSTITUTED / BONDED

QUALITY ★☆☆☆

COMMON APPLICATIONS

Low-cost Garment · Furniture Upholstery

- Can either have a smooth full grain or synthetic grain appearance
- Shreds of leather straps bond with polyurethane or latex
- Content of leather varies from 10–90%, thus affecting its properties
- Considered faux leather when the leather content percentage is low

(7.5) THICKNESS & APPLICATIONS

Applications depend on the leather's thickness and weight. Ounces are the standard measurement unit of leather weight.

THICKNESS	OZ.	IRONS	DECIMAL	INCHES	MM.	COMMON APPLICATIONS
	1	0.75	0.0156	1/64	0.4	Jackets — Embossing — Furniture
	2	1.50	0.0313	1/32	0.8	
	3	2.25	0.0469	3/64	1.2	
	4	3.00	0.0625	1/16	1.6	Clutches — Billfold Backs — Embossing
	5	3.75	0.0781	5/64	2.0	Handbags — Clutches — Embossing
	6	4.50	0.0938	3/32	2.4	Handbags — Notebook Covers
	7	5.25	0.1094	7/64	2.8	Carved Handbags — Camera Cases — Journal Covers
	8	6.00	0.125	1/8	3.2	Narrow Belts — Small Holsters — Knife Sheaths
	9	6.75	0.1406	9/64	3.6	Belts — Holsters
	10	7.50	0.1563	5/32	4.0	Wider Belts — Heavier Holsters

7.6 COMMON TANNING METHODS

Tanning is a process that turns the skin into leather. It involves treatment that stabilizes the protein structure and prevents bacteria, putrefaction, and possibly coloration.

VEGETABLE-TANNED LEATHER

Tannins from the leaves and bark of plants bind to the collagen protein in the hide or skin. The whole process takes roughly 40 to 60 days. A more sustainable option, it is less water-soluble and more resistant to bacteria.

CHROME-TANNED LEATHER

Also known as "wet blue", chrome tanning is the most common tanning method. It uses a solution of chemicals, acids, and salts. The process can be finished in a day, which is much quicker than vegetable tanning. Various colors are available.

LATIGO-TANNED LEATHER

Also known as semi-vegetable tanning, this combines the vegetable- and chrome-tanning processes. Applied to heavyweight hides, mostly cowhides, it first uses the chrome-tanning method, and then the vegetable-tanning method. Latigo-tanned leather is both durable and pliable.

ALDEHYDE-TANNED LEATHER

Sometimes referred to as "wet white", aldehyde tanning is typically used for the leather in automobiles and the shoes of infants, with glutaraldehyde or oxazolidine compounds being used to tan the hides or skins.

RAWHIDE

Rawhide is made by soaking the skin in lime and stretching it before the drying process. Due to the stiffness and brittleness, it can be cut into cord and made into shoelaces.

OIL-TANNED LEATHER

Oil tanning typically uses fish oil after the initial vegetable tanning process. The oil content makes the leather softer and more pliable. Oil-tanned leather is common in shoemaking.

(7.7) LEATHER SOURCE

CATTLE & CALF

CATTLE

CALF

MEASURED AREA

Cattle: 35 - 55 sq.ft
Calf: 10 -18 sq.ft

CHARACTERISTICS

Stiff but breaks easily

COMMON APPLICATIONS

Outerwear, Bags, and Shoes

The most common leather source with obvious rough grain across the whole hide. Calfskin, a lightweight leather made from young cattle, has a finer grain that is softer and smoother than the leather from cows or bulls. *Note: Bull leather usually has a finer grain than cow leather.*

PIGSKIN

MEASURED AREA

-

CHARACTERISTICS

Flexible due to the high lanolin content

COMMON APPLICATIONS

Suede, Shoe Insoles, Linings

A durable, soft leather with an obvious tight grain and pores. It is usually supple and rubbery.

SHEEP & LAMB

SHEEP

SHEEP

LAMB

LAMB

MEASURED AREA	CHARACTERISTICS
Sheep: 5 - 15 sq.ft / Lamb: 3 - 5 sq.ft / Bigger lamb: 5 - 7 sq.ft	Delicate but flexible

COMMON APPLICATIONS

All kinds of applications

A lightweight, fine-grained leather with a loose, fibrous texture. Baby lamb leather is soft, "buttery", and supple to the touch, with a finer grain.

GOAT

MEASURED AREA	CHARACTERISTICS
3 - 5 sq.ft	High tensile strength

COMMON APPLICATIONS

Often used for suede across all kinds of applications

A wild leather that is soft and supple, with a fine grain. It usually has more defects on its surface than sheep leather.

ALLIGATOR

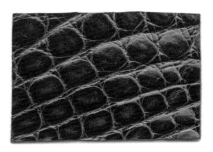

MEASURED AREA

Calculated by measuring four scutes in a group from edge to edge

Length: 50cm upwards

CHARACTERISTICS

Durable due to the scute layer in the skin

COMMON APPLICATIONS

Suede, Watch Straps, Bags

A soft, supple leather with an uneven flat scute. The leather is thick at the sides and thin at the belly and limbs.

SNAKE

MEASURED AREA

Width x length

CHARACTERISTICS

Flexible due to thinness

COMMON APPLICATIONS

Apparel, Accessories, Shoes, Belts, Boots, Handbags

A soft, smooth, and ridged patterned leather with a hexagonal scute across the ventral area. Back and front cuts available.

OSTRICH

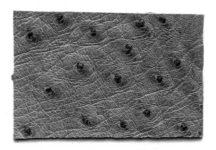

MEASURED AREA

16 sq.ft

CHARACTERISTICS

-

COMMON APPLICATIONS

Boots, Trimmings, Accessories

A soft, smooth, grainy, and thick leather with a raised circular texture.

KANGAROO

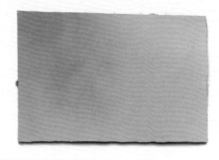

THICKNESS	CHARACTERISTICS
< 0.8 - 1mm	• High tensile strength • Higher abrasion resistance than cowhide and goatskin

COMMON APPLICATIONS

Upholstery, Shoes (such as military boots, football boots), Accessories

A soft, suede-like leather with a smooth surface that usually has fur on the back.

EEL

MEASURED AREA	CHARACTERISTICS
-	Thin but very durable

COMMON APPLICATIONS

Upholstery, Apparel, Accessories, Wallets, Handbags

A shiny, soft, thin leather formed of small patches with a vertical stripe down the middle.

DEERSKIN

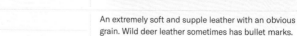

MEASURED AREA	CHARACTERISTICS
-	High tensile strength and abrasion resistance

COMMON APPLICATIONS

Lightweight one-piece outerwear

An extremely soft and supple leather with an obvious grain. Wild deer leather sometimes has bullet marks.

STINGRAY

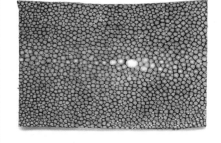

MEASURED AREA	CHARACTERISTICS
0.8 sq.ft	Flame resistant, with a siliceous layer

COMMON APPLICATIONS

Bags, Wallets

A smooth, durable, and rigid leather with tiny round bumps.

HAND FEEL: Coated, smooth

LIZARD

WIDTH	CHARACTERISTICS
20 - 30cm	Waterproof

COMMON APPLICATIONS

Wallets, Trimmings

A papery, grainy textured leather with a shiny, small scute on the surface.

HORSE

MEASURED AREA	CHARACTERISTICS
-	• High tensile strength • Regulates temperature

COMMON APPLICATIONS

Shoes, Belts

A smooth, thick leather with a fine grain on the surface. Usually the back of the horse has better leather than the front of the horse. Only four manufacturers in the world produce horsehide.

(7.8) FAUX/ ARTIFICIAL LEATHER

Faux leather, sometimes referred to as leatherette, pleather, or vegan leather, is an alternative to animal leather.

COMMON MATERIALS	
PU FAUX LEATHER FABRIC	**PVC FAUX LEATHER FABRIC**
PU faux leather, also called bicast or bycast leather, is a woven- or non-woven-based faux leather made from fibrous leather that is coated or laminated with a 100% PU (polyurethane) finishing.	PVC faux leather is a vinyl synthetic leather made of polyvinyl chloride with added plasticizers, which sits on a woven or non-woven fabric.

ADVANTAGES & DISADVANTAGES	
• Easy to cut and sew • Less noticeable needle marks • Consistent appearance • Easier to dye with various colors than animal leather • Lower price	▲ Unbreathable ▲ Unstretchable ▲ Easy to tear, and peels over time

COMPARING NATURAL LEATHER & FAUX LEATHER	FAUX LEATHER	NATURAL LEATHER
REVERSE SIDE OF THE MATERIAL	Textile back, plastic coated	Fibrous back
GRAIN PATTERN	Uniform surface	Irregular
CUTTING EDGE	Smooth and clean edge 	Lint-like edge with dense fiber layer
SMELL	Odorless	Earthy and slightly sweet
BREATHABILITY	Non-breathable	Breathable
HEAT REACTION	Melts and burns well; smells like burnt plastic	Glows and solidifies; smells like burnt hair

⑦.⑨ FAUX FUR

Faux fur, also known as pile fabric, is designed to resemble animal fur. It is usually made from acrylic polymers and is processed, dyed, and cut to create specific fur textures by weaving, tufting, circular looping, or knitting fibers into the backing fabric.

COMMON MATERIALS

FUR FIBERS

Acrylic / Modacrylic / Silk / Wool / Mohair

FUR BACKING

Cotton / Wool / Polypropylene (PP)

PRODUCTION TECHNIQUES

WEAVING

Looping fibers through the backing fabric to interlace two parts. The technique can produce a wide range of fabrics.

TUFTING

A similar method to weaving, but at a higher speed.

CIRCULAR LOOPING & KNITTING

Using the same technique as plain knitting to produce faux fur, it is the most economical and fastest production technique.

ADVANTAGES & DISADVANTAGES

- Low production cost and more affordable than animal fur
- More ethical, since no animals are used
- Anti-microbial and more durable with proper care
- Easier to handle during the production process and maintenance

▲ Environmental unfriendly, as the materials used to create faux fur are non-biodegradable
▲ Less insulating than animal fur, and less breathable

COMPAREING ANIMAL FUR & FAUX FUR	ANIMAL FUR	FAUX FUR
BURN TEST	Singes and smells like burnt hair	Melts and smells like burnt plastic
CONSTRUCTION	Skin-based	Webbing-based
TIP OF FIBERS	Natural hair, pointed	Machine-cut, united
PIN TEST	Hard to pass through	Easy to pass through

FINISH -ING

08

A finishing process is an additional chemical or mechanical treatment applied to change a fabric's appearance or properties.

200 ↓ 223

A finishing process is often used to change the aesthetic or function of a fabric, including printing and dyeing. Different finishings can be applied at different stages of production, with the outcome of each finishing depending on the textile.

(8.1) TYPES OF DYE

Different coloring agents will be used depending on the type of fibers, fabric constructions, expected results, required colorfastness, costs and water/energy consumption issues.

DYE	DESCRIPTION	SUITABLE FIBERS
Acid	• Easy application • Complete color range with good bright shades	Wool, Silk, Nylon
Azoic	• Complicated application • Economical • Limited color range, best on red • Prohibited in EU market	Mainly Cotton and Cellulosic
Basic	• Easy application for acrylics • Complete and brilliant color range • Poor fastness on cellulosic	Acrylic
Direct	• Simple application • Cheap • Complete color range • Duller than basic or acid	Mainly Cellulosic, Silk, Rayon, Wool
Disperse	• Known as acetate dyes • Skill required in application • Economical • Complete color range	Acetate, Polyester, Nylon, Acrylic
Mordant (Chrome)	• Complicated application • Expensive • Complete but dull color range	Wool, Silk, Cellulosic, Acrylic
Reactive	• Easy application • Economical • Complete color range • Good fastness (increased use in printing)	Cotton and Cellulosic Fiber, Wool, Silk, Rayon
Sulphur	• Complicated application • Cheap • Incomplete color range (no bright shades)	Cellulosic
Vat	• Complicated application • Most expensive • Incomplete shade range • Best all-around fastness	Cotton
Metal Complex	• Complicated application • Expensive • Complete color range • Duller than acid	Wool, Nylon

RESISTANCE TO LIGHT	RESISTANCE TO WASHING	RESISTANCE TO PERSPIRATION	RESISTANCE TO RUBBING	RESISTANCE TO DRY-CLEANING
★★★	★	★★	★★★★	★★★
★★★	★★★	★★★	★★	★★
★★★	★★★	★★★	★★★	★★★
★★	★★	★★★	★★★	★★★
★★★	★★★	★★★	★★★	★★★
★★★★	★★★	★★★	★★★	★★★
★★★	★★★	★★★★	★★★	★★★
★★★	★★★	★★★	★★★★	★★★★
★★★★	★★★★	★★★★	★★★	★★★
★★★★	★★★	★★★	★★★★	★★★

(8.2) STAGES OF DYEING

Dyeing can be done at all stages of textile manufacturing. The method should be chosen in accordance with the type of fabric or garment being produced.

STOCK DYEING / TOP DYEING

The dyeing of loose, unspun fibers, also known as stock or wool fibers. The shorter fibers, known as top fibers, should be removed before they are spun into yarn.

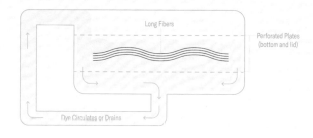

DOPE DYEING / SOLUTION PIGMENTING

Specifically used for filament fibers where dyes are added to the spinning solution before extracting the filaments.

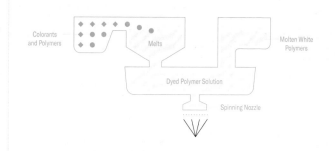

YARN DYEING

Yarn dyeing is done after the fibers are spun into yarn and before it is woven or knitted into fabric. Commonly used in multicolored or patterned designs, yarn dyeing comes in different forms, such as skein, package, and beam.

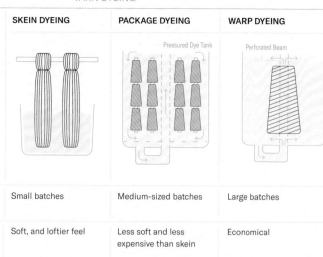

	SKEIN DYEING	PACKAGE DYEING	WARP DYEING
QUANTITY OF YARN	Small batches	Medium-sized batches	Large batches
CHARACTERISTICS	Soft, and loftier feel	Less soft and less expensive than skein	Economical

FABRIC / PIECE DYEING

Fabric dyeing takes place after the weaving and knitting process. It is the most popular and flexible dyeing method for solid colors. The methods used for this type of dyeing include jet, jig, pad, and beam dyeing.

JET DYEING

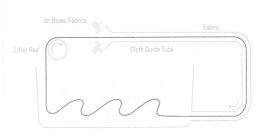

Jet Blows Fabrics

Fabric

Lifter Reel

Cloth Guide Tube

JIG DYEING

Fabric

PAD DYEING

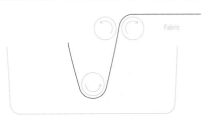

Fabric

GARMENT DYEING

Garment dyeing is the dyeing of completed garments. It is an economical method for dyeing non-tailored and simpler forms such as sweaters and T-shirts. Tailored items, which can be easily distorted and shrunk, are not recommended for garment dyeing.

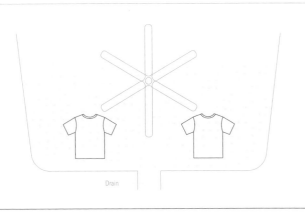

Drain

(8.3) PRINTING METHODS

		COLOR LIMITATIONS
ROLLER PRINTING Patterns are printed by engraved metal (mostly copper) rollers		Within 5 colors
SCREEN PRINTING Prints pattern by spreading ink across the stencil screen with the aid of a blade or squeegee.	**A. FLATBED SCREEN PRINTING:** Also known as silkscreen printing, as the screen was often made of silk in the past. 	6-8 colors
	B. ROTARY SCREEN PRINTING: Similar to flatbed screen printing, but uses a rotary screen with a squeegee inside. 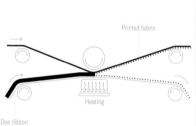	10-12 colors
TRANSFER PRINTING Designs are first printed onto a nontextile substrate, then transferred to the textile by a separate process, usually a heat press.	**A. SUBLIMATION PRINTING:** Sublimation dyes sublime from the paper and diffuse into a textile by heat press.	—
	B. FILM RELEASE: Polymer/PU film is transferred from the paper to the textile with the aid of a heat press. 	—
	C. HEAT TRANSFER (DIGITAL): Uses a heat press machine to apply the design.	—
DIGITAL PRINTING Overall garment print. Print is computerized and applied using an inkjet.		—

PRODUCTION MINIMUM	PRINT PRODUCTS	FIBER RESTRICTIONS	ADVANTAGES	DISADVANTAGES
High order minimum	Rolls of fabric	—	• Good for repetitive designs • Able to print continuous vertical lines or patterns without joining lines • High production speed	• Width and pattern repetition restricted by the length and diameter of the roller • High engraving cost for rollers • Not suitable for knitted fabric
Low order minimum	—	—	• Flexible pattern size • Can support different printing agents • Good brightness of color	• Time consuming and costly to develop screens • Low-productivity method
High order minimum	Rolls of fabric	—	• High productivity • Able to print continuous vertical lines and patterns without joining lines • Can support different printing agents • Good brightness of color	• Width and pattern repetition restricted by the length and diameter of the roller • Time consuming and costly to develop screens • Not suitable for fine and delicate patterns
Low order minimum	Fabric	Mainly polyester	• Minimum use of water and chemicals • Excellent sharpness of design	• Limited choices of fabric materials • Special printing paper and dyes are needed
Low order minimum	Pieces of fabric or garment	—	• Excellent sharpness of design • Various types of transfer paper are available on the market	• Pattern area is stiff due to the dyeing agent; this affects breathability • Special printing paper and dyes are needed
Low order minimum	Pieces of fabric or garment	—	• Excellent sharpness of design • Very short development time • Suitable for photogenic prints	• Pattern area is stiff due to the dyeing agent; this affects breathability • Special printing paper and dyes are needed
Low order minimum	Pieces of fabric or garment	Avoid cotton	• Convenient for communication • Short development time and lead time • Suitable for photogenic prints • Excellent sharpness of design • Wide color range available	• High in capital • Special ink is needed • Fair colorfastness • Restricted by the number of machines available

(8.4) PRINTING STYLES

DIRECT PRINTING

Direct printing is the most popular and straightforward style; patterns are printed directly onto the fabric.

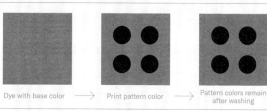

Dye with base color ⟶ Print pattern color ⟶ Pattern colors remain after washing

DISCHARGE PRINTING

Discharge printing, also called extract printing, is commonly used for printing fine and sharp designs, or printing light colors on dark fabric. Instead of ink, a color-destroying agent is applied to the fabric to remove or lighten the dye. This printing style works best on cotton fabrics.

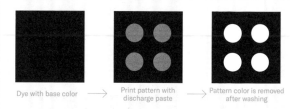

Dye with base color ⟶ Print pattern with discharge paste ⟶ Pattern color is removed after washing

RESIST PRINTING

Resist printing has a similar effect to discharge printing. In this method, an area of the fabric is pre-treated with a dye-resistant paste or wax. When the fabric is dyed, the treated area remains undyed, resulting in a pattern on the fabric.

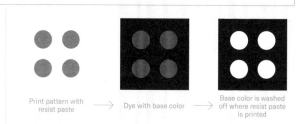

Print pattern with resist paste ⟶ Dye with base color ⟶ Base color is washed off where resist paste is printed

(8.5) COLORFASTNESS

Colorfastness refers to the ability of the dye to retain its color. The degree of color resistance to fading or running is measured in four main ways:

Light Fastness

Color loss from exposure to light (UV rays)

Gas Fastness

Color loss from dry-cleaning

Wash Fastness

Color loss in water

Rub Fastness

Color loss due to abrasion or rubbing – can be tested by wet and dry crocking

LAB DIP

Lab dip or lab dye is a small piece of fabric, often called a test swatch, which is dyed a particular shade according to the buyer's requirements. Lab-dip approval is required from a buyer before bulk production.

DYE LOTS

Every dye lot will be slightly different, and it is impossible to achieve the same color from different dye baths, or even different dye batches, since variations can easily occur during the dyeing process.

(8.6) FIXING STEPS

FIXATION

A process to stabilize the dye and size of fabric.

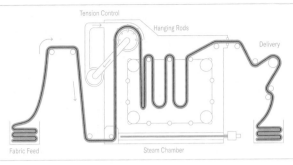

Tension Control
Hanging Rods
Delivery
Fabric Feed
Steam Chamber

WASHING

A treatment that is used to remove impurities and oils, and stabilize sizing during the finishing stage.

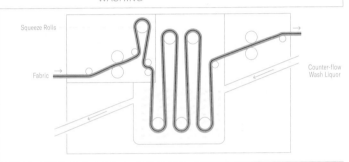

Squeeze Rolls
Fabric
Counter-flow Wash Liquor

DEWATERING AND DRYING

A treatment to reduce the wetness of the fabric after the wetting process.

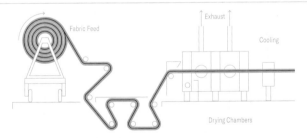

Fabric Feed
Exhaust
Cooling
Drying Chambers

HEAT SETTING

A process to remove irregular appearances and stabilize the dimensions of heat-sensitive fibers, yarns, or fabrics.

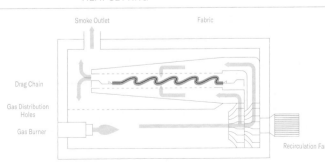

Smoke Outlet
Fabric
Drag Chain
Gas Distribution Holes
Gas Burner
Recirculation Fan

(8.7) FINISHING SCHEDULE

Different finishing steps might be taken by different finishing companies to achieve similar results. Below is a common schedule for printed or dyed fabric.

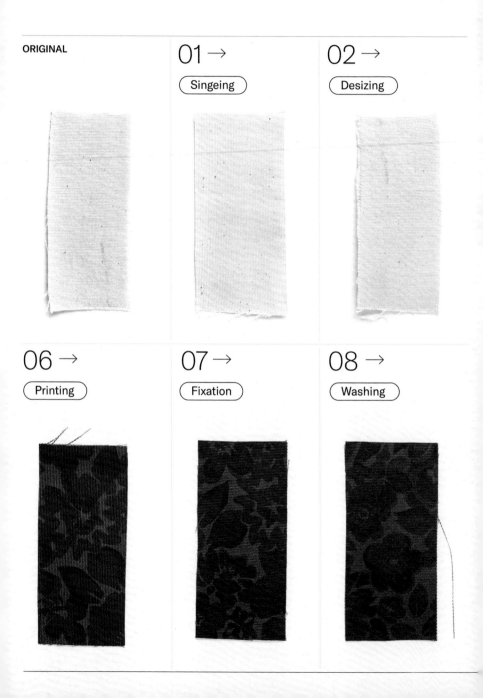

ORIGINAL

01 → Singeing

02 → Desizing

06 → Printing

07 → Fixation

08 → Washing

03 →
(Bleaching)

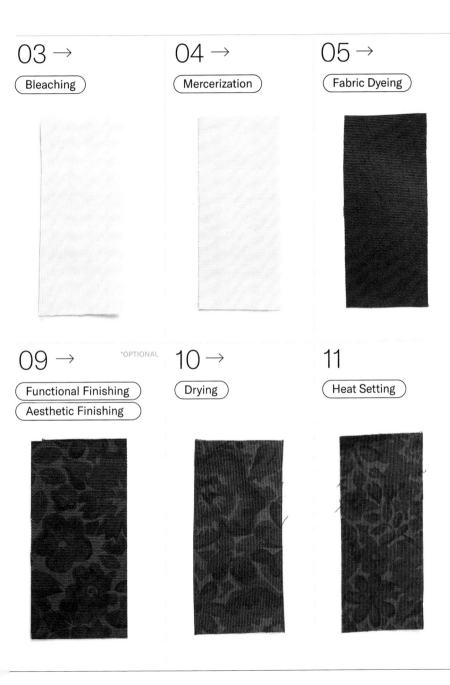

04 →
(Mercerization)

05 →
(Fabric Dyeing)

09 →   *OPTIONAL
(Functional Finishing)
(Aesthetic Finishing)

10 →
(Drying)

11
(Heat Setting)

SIZING

Applies a protective coating to warp yarn to increase abrasion resistance, weavability, and minimize yarn breakage during the weaving process.

→ Chemical
→ Temporary

Remarks: Sizing agent differs depending on the fiber, spinning methods, and thickness of the yarn.

DESIZING

Breaking down the "*size*" of the warp yarn during the fabric stage to increase the absorbency, dyeing, and printing ability.

→ Chemical
→ Permanent

SINGEING

Pre-treatment to provide a smooth and uniform fabric surface by burning off loose fiber ends.

→ Mechanical
→ Permanent

Remarks: Cellulose fibers are easily singed, while thermoplastic fibers are harder to singe as they can melt and harden under heat.

SCOURING

A pre-treatment using an alkali to remove natural or added impurities (such as oil, fat, and wax) for better bleaching, dyeing, and printing ability.

→ Mechanical
→ Permanent

BLEACHING

→ Chemical
→ Permanent

Treatment to remove natural fiber color
with the help of bleaching agents. Bleached
materials are usually white, which is better for
the subsequent dyeing and printing processes.

MERCERIZING

→ Chemical
→ Permanent

*Remarks: Usually
applied to cotton yarn
or fabric*

Treatment to increase smoothness, luster, and
absorbency. The treatment can be carried
out during both the yarn and fabric stage by
immersing the material in sodium hydroxide.

TENTERING

→ Mechanical
→ Temporary

A tenter frame stretches fabric and sets the
warp and weft at right angles. The fabric
then passes through a heated chamber that
removes wrinkles, straightens the weave
and dries fabric to its final size.

BEETLING

→ Mechanical
→ Permanent

Beetling produces a firm, smooth, high-gloss,
linen-like cellulosic fabric by hammering it
with wooden mallets called "*beetlers*".

FULLING

→ Mechanical
→ Permanent

Fulling, also known as tucking or walking, increases the thickness and compactness of woven or knitted wool by subjecting it to shrinkage of 10–25% in an environment of heat and moisture.

WEIGHTING

→ Mechanical
→ Temporary

Remarks: Excessive metallic salt will weaken the fabric, resulting in cracking and splitting during use.

Weighting adds additional weight to silk by immersing it in metallic salts, thus improving drapability and hand feel.

SILICONE

→ Chemical
→ Permanent

A silicone coating treatment creates a silky texture and adds protective and insulating properties to the fabric.

SOFTENING

→ Chemical
→ Temporary

Softening creates a sleek and smooth surface, primarily to improve the softness of a fabric.

CALENDERING

→ Mechanical

Calendering compresses the fabric to smooth, flatten, reduce thickness, and create luster.

01A. EMBOSSING

01B. DEBOSSING

02. MOIRE

03. GLAZING & CIRE

01. EMBOSSING / DEBOSSING

→ Mechanical
→ Permanent

A finishing process that creates a lowered or raised decorative surface in the fabric.

EMBOSSING: A raised 3D form on a fabric, where a layer of polymer stiffener is introduced to increase the durability of the embossing effect.

DEBOSSING: A lowered form pressed into the fabric using high temperatures.

02. MOIRÉ

→ Mechanical
→ Permanent

A treatment to give a distinct watery or wave-shaped pattern to a ribbed fabric by passing folded material through ribbed or engraved rollers at high temperatures.

03. GLAZING & CIRE

→ Mechanical
→ Permanent or Temporary

A treatment adding luster and smoothness to the surface of a fabric by calendering in a starch, wax, and resin solution.

04. SCHREINERING

→ Mechanical
→ Temporary or Durable

A treatment creating reflection, soft luster, and a silk-like appearance by making fine rib lines on the surface of the fabric.

NAPPING AND BRUSHING

Napping and brushing use brushes to raise the fibers and create a nap, which also softens the surface. Napped fabric traps air, providing warmth.

→ Mechanical
→ Permanent

SANDING AND SUEDING

Sanding, also called sueding or peach finishing, is a process that produces a suede-like surface by abrading the fibers.

→ Mechanical
→ Permanent

SHEARING

A treatment to smooth and even out the surface of piled fabric. It can also create patterns and improve the color of the fabric.

→ Mechanical
→ Permanent

FLOCKING

A treatment to create pile, a raised
surface, or imitate extra yarn weave
by adhering fiber onto a base fabric.
Shedding may occur, because not all
fibers adhere to the adhesive.

→ Mechanical
→ Permanent

BURNOUT

This expensive treatment, also called
devoré, is usually applied to velvet to
create a semi-transparent pattern by
applying acid to dissolve fibers.

→ Chemical
→ Permanent

PLEATING

A treatment to create systematic
folds in the fabric.

→ Mechanical
→ Temporary

PLISSÉ

A treatment creating wrinkles within vertical stripes on a fabric surface by shrinking the fabric in particular areas.

→ Chemical
→ Permanent

EMBROIDERY

A decorative finishing that uses different stitches, yarns, and materials to create patterns on the fabric.

→ Mechanical
→ Permanent

FOIL PRINT

A treatment that creates a metallic graphic by pressing metallic paper (foil) onto the fabric using heat.

→ Mechanical
→ Durable

PUFF PRINT

Puff printing, also known as embossing, is a raised or 3D colored print on a textile surface created using a foaming agent.

→ Chemical
→ Durable

QUILTING

A thick padded material created by stitching three layers together: top quilting, insulating material, and backing material. The thick layers also help retain warmth.

01. DENSE QUILT

→ Mechanical
→ Permanent

A tighter quilting that is more durable and long-lasting. Often used when creating more complicated patterns.

DENIM FINISHING

Treatments are used to enhance
the appeal of denim to achieve a
fashionable look.

→ Mechanical
→ Chemical
→ Permanent

Influential factors: There is no standard for denim washing.
The outcome of denim finishing depends on the washing cycle,
water amount, types of fabric, and machine.

RAW DENIM

01. RINSE WASHING

Also known as dark wash, most
basic wash for denim.

→Chemical

02. BLEACHING

Decoloring or whitening
the fabric.

→Chemical

03. ENZYME WASHING

Breaking down and weakening
the fabric surface.

→Chemical

04. PP SPRAY / MONKEY WASHING

A color-fading effect
achieved by spraying on
an oxidizing agent.

→Chemical

05. TINTING / OVERDYEING

A dyeing process that
tints clothes after the
fading process.

→Chemical

06. OZONE FADING

Chemical bleaching due to
an oxidative reaction with
indigo dye.

→Chemical

01. RINSE WASHED

02. BLEACHED

03. ENZYME WASHED

04. PP SPRAYED / MONKEY WASHED

05. TINTED / OVERDYED

07. SANDWASHED / SANDBLASTED

09. STONEWASHED

10. ACID WASHED

12. CRUSH FINISHED

07. SANDWASHING / SANDBLASTING

A de-coloring process done manually or mechanically by applying abrasive material under pressure. The process can be deadly to workers.

→ Abrasion

08. WATERJET FADING

A mechanical treatment using hydro jets to wash out the dye of a fabric.

→ Abrasion

09. STONEWASHING

A physical, mechanical treatment to achieve a worn appearance.

→ Abrasion

10. ACID WASHING

Also known as marble, moon, or snow washing, acid washing is a mix of chemical and mechanical washing to produce a snowy, faded pattern.

→ Abrasion

11. LASERING

A mechanical dry finishing process that uses laser treatment to create a faded effect, or design artwork and logos.

→ Other

12. CRUSH FINISHING

A 3D wrinkled or crushed effect created by spraying or dipping fabric into a resin solution.

→ Other

SANFORIZATION

→ Mechanical
→ Permanent

An anti-shrinkage treatment used to stabilize and minimize the shrinkage of fabric. Shrink-control finishing for wool is called decatizing.

WRINKLE RESISTANCE

→ Chemical
→ Temporary

A treatment using resin to prevent fabric from wrinkling. Resistance tends to loosen after 25 to 30 washes.

FLAME RETARDANT/ FLAME RESISTANCE

→ Chemical
→ Temporary

A treatment to improve self-extinguishing properties by adding a crisp, non-penetrating coating that is able to cut off oxygen.

MOISTURE WICKING

→ Chemical
→ Permanent

A treatment to pull sweat or moisture outside of a fabric by weaving hydrophilic fibers into hydrophobic fibers, or changing the structure of synthetic fiber into structured trilobal fibers.

DURABLE WATER REPELLENT (DWR)

A treatment that coats the exterior shell of a fabric or infuses the fibers, helping prevent water absorption or penetration. Retreatment is needed to maintain water repellency.

→ Mechanical
→ Temporary or Permanent

Remarks: Retreatment is needed to maintain water repellency.

WATER RESISTANT

A treatment resisting the contact of a light amount of water.

WATER REPELLENT

A treatment that repels water on contact. It is considered hydrophobic.

WATERPROOF

A treatment that repels water on contact. Considered hydrophobic, it provides the most water protection of the three.

Levels of Water Protection:
1. Waterproof
2. Water repellent
3. Water resistant

ANTI-STATIC

A treatment to remove unwanted static charge generated during body movements or fabric friction by applying an anti-static agent.

→ Chemical
→ Durable or Non-durable

ANTI-PILLING

A treatment reducing loose fibers on a fabric's surface to avoid the formation of little balls, pills, or threads. A polymeric coating is usually applied to the fabric's surface to make it more durable.

→ Chemical
→ Durable

UV PROTECTION

→ Chemical
→ Durable

A treatment to reduce fabric exposure to UV rays through application of a blocking agent that absorbs or scatters the rays.

ORGANIC UV BLOCKER

Used to absorb UV rays, but only suitable for specific applications due to its flammable and toxic characteristics.

INORGANIC UV BLOCKER

Used to scatter UVA and UVB rays. Inorganic agents are non-toxic and more stable under UV radiation than organic agents.

TEMPERATURE REGULATION

→ Chemical
→ Permanent

Also known as thermo-regulation, temperature regulation is a treatment that uses microcapsule chemicals known as phase change materials (PCMs). These can interrupt temperature changes and provide heating or cooling effects in a garment.

SOIL / STAIN REPELLENT

→ Chemical
→ Permanent

A treatment that uses a laminated chemical coating to prevent stains being absorbed into the fabric.

SOIL / STAIN RELEASE

→ Mechanical
→ Durable

A treatment that increases the water absorption of a fabric, allowing stains or dirt to be more easily removed through washing.

MOTH PROOF

→ Chemical
→ Durable

A treatment that uses a solution to reduce the attraction of moths and prevent damage to the garment.

ANTI-MICROBIAL

→ Chemical
→ Temporary

Also known as anti-bacterial or odor control, this treatment inhibits the growth of bacteria to prevent damage due to sweat.

PATTERNS
MOTIFS

—

&

COLORS

—

Graphics or pigmented colors are added to a textile's surface for decorative purposes.

Patterns, motifs, and colors provide meaning and offer a distinctive or fashionable design point of view.

(11.1) STRIPES

PINSTRIPE

A very narrow thin stripe. Usually in white or gray.

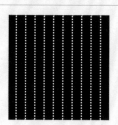

CHALK STRIPE

White or off-white stripe on a dark background. Often used for suits. Wider than pinstripe or pencil stripe.

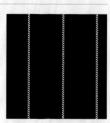

SHARKSKIN (PICK AND PICK)

Diagonal thin lines with narrow spaces.

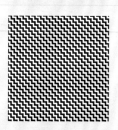

PENCIL STRIPE

Two or three wide warp stripes. Wider than pinstripe but narrower than chalk stripe. Commonly used for shirt fabrics.

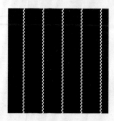

BENGAL

An evenly spaced solid 1/4" stripe on a white background. Commonly used for dress-shirt fabrics.

CANDY STRIPE

An evenly spaced solid 1/8" stripe on a white background.

SHADOW STRIPE

Vertical colored stripe parallel with shadow.

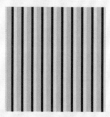

AWNING (CABANA STRIPE)

An evenly spaced solid 1/2" stripe on a white background. Often used for outdoor awning fabrics.

ROPE STRIPE

A wider chalk stripe with lines resembling rope.

(11.2) GEOMETRIC

HERRINGBONE

V-shape lined pattern resembles herring bones. Rows slope in opposite directions.

HEXAGON / HONEYCOMB

A six-sided polygon or hexagon pattern.

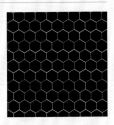

QUATREFOIL

An outline of 4 overlapping circles. A popular pattern during the Gothic and Renaissance eras.

FRET

A band or border of consistent lines that meet at the same angle.

ARGYLE

Formed using different-colored diamonds overlapping with diagonal lines. Often used for sweaters and ties.

DOT

A pattern of dots.

BIRDSEYE

A pattern formed of small diamonds with dots in the middle.

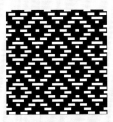

NAILHEAD

Features little square dots on a dark background. Commonly used in tailored suits.

SCALE

A repeating motif resembling fish scales.

(11.3) CHECKERED

GRAPH CHECK

A check resembling a mathematics graph pattern.

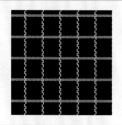

GLEN PLAID

Irregular small and large checks form a pattern with a twill design. Often used on woolen fabric. Popular for suiting.

PIN CHECK

Single colored pin-sized stripes cross each other to form a checked pattern.

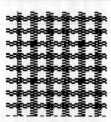

MINI CHECK

A small check pattern between the size of a pin check and a gingham check.

WINDOWPANE

Thin stripes spaced wide apart cross each other on warp and weft yarn. Resembles the panes of a window.

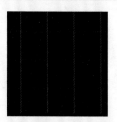

HOUNDSTOOTH

A broken, 4-point geometric pattern that resembles a hound's tooth. Usually in black and white.

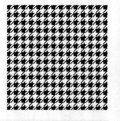

SHEPHERD'S CHECK

A twill weave-based check pattern similar to gingham. Usually in black and white.

TATTERSALL

Thin and regularly spaced stripes form squares that alternate between two colors on a light-colored base.

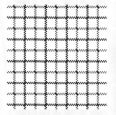

GINGHAM

A check pattern formed with solid, transparent, and light-colored squares on a white background.

TARTAN

Various colored stripes with diagonal lines on weft and warp yarns cross each other and form a multicolored check.

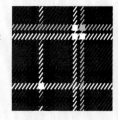

ROYAL STEWART TARTAN

A tartan pattern associated with the Royal House of Stewart. Personal tartan of Queen Elizabeth II.

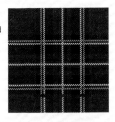

BURBERRY CHECK

Signature check of luxury fashion house Burberry.

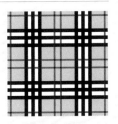

CLAN WALLACE

Also known as "Wallace Red". Best associated with the brand 3M.

BLACK WATCH TARTAN

A green and blue check tartan. Used for the Royal Regiment of Scotland.

MADRAS

A colored check often using bright palettes, including orange, pink, blue, and yellow.

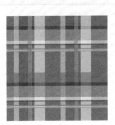

BUFFALO

A large, square check formed using different colors. Mainly red and black.

(11.4) PATTERN: OTHERS

CAMOUFLAGE

CAMOUFLAGE

A pattern used to blend into the environment, often in natural colors.

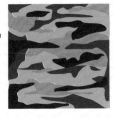

PLANTS

PAISLEY

A teardrop-shaped motif consisting of different decorative graphics inside.

VINTAGE FLORAL

A historical floral pattern.

CALICO

A bright-colored, small-scale floral pattern. Usually associated with American country-style fabric.

SCROLL

A pattern featuring spirals and curved vine and floral elements.

DITSY

Formed with small random prints including spots and flowers.

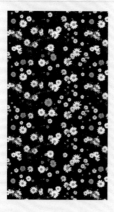

TROPICAL

Pattern consisting of banana leaves or palm trees and flowers.

ANIMALS

CHEETAH

Solid black spots on a yellow-brown background imitate a cheetah skin.

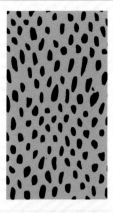

ZEBRA

Irregular black and white lines imitate the pattern of a zebra skin.

GIRAFFE

Large brown patches on a light yellow-brown background imitate a giraffe skin.

LEOPARD

Horseshoe-shaped black patches with brown spots in the center imitate a leopard skin.

TIGER

An orange background with black irregular lines imitate a tiger skin.

(11.5) COLORS

| | | YELLOW | | |

IVORY	CORN SILK / PALE CADMIUM YELLOW	LEMON CHIFFON	CREAM	LIGHT JASMINE YELLOW
NAPLES YELLOW	DAFFODIL	CANARY YELLOW	LEMON	JASMINE YELLOW / ACID YELLOW
SWEETCORN	MIMOSA	CHROME YELLOW	ARYLIDE YELLOW	SULPHUR YELLOW
WHEAT	DEEP CHROME YELLOW	GOLD	CITRINE YELLOW	VEGAS GOLD
ANTIQUE GOLD	SAFFRON AMBOGE	GOLDEN ROCK / YELLOW OCHRE	AMBER	OLIVE OCHRE

BROWN

SAND	HAZELNUT	VANILLA	BEIGE	FLAX
MAUVE BROWN	CAMEL	GOLDEN OAK	BURLYWOOD	KHAKI
TAN	GINGER	CARAMEL	CINNAMON	BRONZE
DARK CHOCOLATE	MAPLE BROWN	PECAN	COYOTE BROWN	DEEP KHAKI
BURNT UMBER	MADDER BROWN	RAW SIENNA	CHESTNUT	VAN DYKE BROWN

[11.5] COLORS

RED

BABY PINK	QUEEN PINK	CHERRY BLOSSOM	SALMON PINK	MISTY ROSE
HOT PINK	AMARANTH PINK	CAMEO PINK	ROSE	CORAL PINK
MAGENTA	CERISE	ALIZARIN CRIMSON	SCARLET	GRAPEFRUIT
FUCHSIA	ROSE MADDER	GUARDSMAN RED	CARMINE	VERMILION
DEEP MAGENTA	WINE	BURGUNDY	MULBERRY	MAROON RED

ORANGE

BISQUE	CHAMPAGNE	MAGNOLIA	NAVAJO	PALE CADMIUM ORANGE
ROSE GOLD	NAPLES YELLOW REDDISH	MELLOW ORANGE	RAJAH	MOCCASIN
TERRA COTTA	PEACH	APRICOT	CADMIUM ORANGE	CHROME TITANATE
CLAY	SUNSET ORANGE	PAPAYA	TANGERINE	FAWN
BRICK	MADDER BROWN	TAWNY	ALLOY ORANGE	MARMALADE

[11.5] COLORS

GREEN

EGGSHELL / PALE PEAR	LIME	PALE JADE	LAUREL GREEN	MINT

CITRON	CHARTREUSE	YELLOW GREEN / APPLE GREEN	SEA GREEN	GLAUCOUS GREEN

PEAR	DAIQUIRI GREEN	CADMIUM GREEN	SHAMROCK GREEN	PALE TEAL

STRAW	OLIVINE	LEAF GREEN	HOOKER'S GREEN	MYRTLE GREEN

OLIVE	OLIVE GREEN / MOSS GREEN	SAP GREEN	FOREST GREEN	VIRIDIAN

BLUE

SEAFOAM	AQUA	PALE SKY	BABY BLUE / PALE BLUE	PALE PERIWINKLE
POWDER BLUE	AQUAMARINE	SKY BLUE	CERULEAN BLUE	CORNFLOWER BLUE
MARINE BLUE	TURQUOISE / EMERALD	CAPRI	STEEL BLUE	ROYAL BLUE
AIR FORCE BLUE	COBALT TEAL	MANGANESE BLUE	INDIGO	COBALT BLUE / SAPPHIRE
TWILIGHT BLUE / DARK SLATE BLUE	LAPIS BLUE	PRUSSIAN BLUE	NAVY	ULTRAMARINE

[11.5] COLORS

PURPLE

HEATHER	BLUEBELL	HYACINTH	PALE ORCHID	LIGHT LILAC
GRAYISH LAVENDER / WISTERIA	BLUE IRIS	LAVENDER	ORCHID	LILAC
DULL BLUE VIOLET	ULTRAMARINE VIOLET	VIOLET	RED VIOLET	PURPLE LAKE
OLD LAVENDER	REGALIA	ROYAL PURPLE	DEEP ORCHID	TYRIAN PURPLE
DEEP PURPLE	GRAPE	DIOXAZINE PURPLE	COBALT VIOLET	QUINACRIDONE VIOLET

MONOCHROME

PALE LILAC GRAY	PALE SILVER	LIGHT GAINSBORO GRAY	PLATINUM	ALABASTER
PALE MAUVE GRAY	SILVER	GAINSBORO GRAY	TIMBERWOLF	DEEP ALABASTER
MAUVE GRAY	SLATE GRAY	STONE GRAY	FOG GRAY	BONE
LILAC GRAY	PAYNE'S GRAY	MARENGO	BATTLESHIP GRAY	DEEP OATMEAL
GRAPHITE	CHARCOAL	JET BLACK	IRON GRAY	TAUPE

ACKNOWLEDGEMENTS

Chairman	PENTER YIP
Editor in Chief	CHARLOTTE CHAN
Editor	JANE KWAN
Designer	SAUMAN WONG
Illustrators	SARA CHOW, VIKKI YAU
Photographers	SATGLE KO, JANE KWAN
Copy Editors	BRIDGET BARNETT, LISA BURNETT HILLMAN
	ENGLISH EDITORIAL SOLUTIONS
Consultants	DR. JOSHUA LAW. | Dr. Law Bing Lam (Joshua) has worked in the textile and garment industry for more than 45 years as a purchasing and general manager involved in garment manufacturing, dyeing, and printing. Through distance learning, he acquired a DBA to further enhance his management skills. With extensive knowledge of textile materials, he lectures at various textile institutions around Hong Kong and is always keen on sharing his knowledge with the younger generations. He is currently a consultant at a woven dyeing and printing factory in China.
	RONNIE TUNG | Ronnie Tung is an award-winning fashion design professional based in Asia. However, she does not limit her creativity to simply design. From manufacturing to retail, she works across the industry spectrum to constantly explore new areas. Shamelessly in love with clothes for most of her life, the affection continues unabated.

Contributors		
AMY LEE	ANDY CHEUNG	ARKIN NG
BRIAN TAM	CALVIN TIU	CARLA WONG
CAROL TAO	DAVID YIU	DR. TRAVIS LI
HILL TSE	IRENE LO	JACK LO
JOHN FIDLER	JOHNNIE LAU	JULIE J. Y. CHUN
KARMUEL YOUNG	KENNETH CHOI	KUHEE TAE
LAMMY CHAN	MATTHEW CHENG Y. H.	MEEGAN MA
MEGAN LI	MICHELLE JUNG	MINNIE LAM
MOUNTAIN YAM	NANCY TONG	RACHEL FONG
RINGO LEE	ROSA LO	SAM HO
STEPHON SOONG	SUSANNA SOO	TAK LEE
TANG KWOK WAI	THOMAS KUNG	YANKEE LEUNG
YOYO TSANG	ZOE KWOK	

FABRIC PROVIDERS

MOOD FABRICS | ⊕ **MOODFABRICS.COM** | Mood Fabrics is one of the biggest fabric retailers in the US and is often regarded as an inspirational second home to Project Runway alumni. Proud to be a family-run business that plays a vital role in the fashion industry for over two decades, Mood Fabrics has built its reputation on creativity, honesty, and hard work. It is also ranked as one of "Fashion's 50 Most Powerful" brands by The New York Daily News.

KNIT SOURCES | *Knit Fabrics* | ⊕ **KNITSOURCES.COM** | Established in 2002, Knit Sources is an accredited factory for sweater design and production located in Hong Kong and mainland China. With a wealth of experience in the industry and boasting quality management, the company provides a seamless one-stop service for clients around the world. Offering a wide range of yarns, style development, accessories sourcing, and production, Knit Sources prides itself on delivering products of the highest standards.

SWATCH ON | *Woven Fabrics* | ⊕ **SWATCHON.COM** | SwatchOn is an online fabric marketplace based in Seoul, South Korea. We inspire fashion designers around the world with a rich and diverse selection of fabrics right at their fingertips. We are proud to be able to introduce high-quality local fabrics from 1,000 Korean suppliers and global fashion designers, creating a whole new opportunity and experience for both parties.

KOKUI | *Denim Fabrics* | ⊕ **KOKUIHK.COM** | Kokui Hong Kong-based workshops provide tools, machinery, and equipment to carry out design, pattern creation, testing, washing, and production in Kwun Tong's main office and workshop. A traditional Hong Kong brand with rich experience in clothing, modification, and washing services, Kokui has been active in Hong Kong's garment industry and around the world for many years.

SUIT ARTISAN | *Suiting Fabrics* | ⊕ **WWW.SUITARTISAN.COM** | Suit Artisan offers ready-to-wear business wear for instant wardrobes solutions for the modern gentlemen. The brand was established by a team of menswear experts, each with ten years of professional experience in the international luxury menswear design and development field. Suit Artisan also offers a made-to-measure tailoring service that caters to the various needs of its customers with a belief in simple, direct, fast, to-the-point, and meticulous craftsmanship.

BEMBERG | *Fibers* | ⊕ ASAHI-KASEI.CO.JP/FIBERS/EN/BEMBERG | Bemberg is the only manufacturer of cupro (Bemberg) in the world. It has been expanding its features and applications in the fashion industry by offering the highest-quality services and products to enrich people's hearts and lives.

KLOCKWISE | *Knit Fabrics* | ⊕ klockwisestudio.com ⊕ IG@klockwise.studio | Klockwise is a contemporary knitwear brand which sets out to create romantic designs by combining classic elements with knitting techniques. As a knitwear brand, the adventure of exploring yarns and stitches never ends. Klockwise celebrates knitwear by creating elegant yet comfortable dresses for every memorable moment.

RIGHT LINK KNITWEAR LTD. | *Knit Fabrics* | ⊕ admin@rightlk.com.hk | Right Link Knitting factory is a sweater manufacturer in Hong Kong, combining innovative concepts and ideas with proven knitting techniques. All products range from 3–16 gauge.

FORDRICH (HK) LIMITED | *Leather Swatches* | ⊕ fordrich.com | Fordrich is a leathers and furs trading house that works with Italian and European tanneries. Since 1987, it has provided a wide range of distinctive leathers and furs of the highest quality. Over 1000 types of leathers and furs are displayed in the company's showroom, offering a large selection for clients.

S.NINE BY SUSANNA SOO | *Woven Fabrics* | ⊕ snineonline.com | Launched in 2009, S.Nine by Susanna Soo is a poetic creation – a collection that redefines traditional foundations, embodying both romance and practicality. Designed for the modern woman, S.Nine by Susanna Soo fulfills her need for both style and function, whilst also tapping into her deeper desires. Through the designer's signature draping techniques, the garments impart on women's sense of self-discovery, where confidence embraces romance.

WUXI MAOYUANJI IMPORT AND EXPORT CO., LTD | Founded in 2004, Maoyuanji is located in Wuxi, China and offers reliable fiber manufacturing services. It specializes in quality nylon products, including virgin nylon fiber, recycled nylon fiber, and functional nylon fiber. As a fast-growing company, a new sub-company: Meijing Technology and Junjie Enterprises was established in 2015.

WEBSITE REFERENCES

abbysyarns.com | acc-silicones.com | acornfabrics.com | adenandanais.com | aestheticstories.com | agronomag.com

aksa.com | altiplanoinsulation.com | aphrodite1994.com | aplf.com | aramid.eu | articlesofstyle.com | asahi-kasei.co.jp

asolengin.files.wordpress.com | atlanticleather.is | authenticity50.com | azom.com | barnhardtcotton.net

bartol-impex.hr | batchmens.com | bblackandsons.com | beckettsimonon.com | belmun.com | benaud.fr

bespokeedge.com | bigduckcanvas.com | biocote.com | blacksheepwools.com | blog.fabricuk.com

blog.madisonavenuecouture.com | blog.paradisefibers.com | blog.plushaddict.co.uk | blog.sternandstern.com

blogaash.blogspot.com | blokesbags.co.uk | britannica.com | britexfabrics.com | buckskinleather.com

buffalojackson.com | bugis.fr | businessoffashion.com | cableknittingstitches.com | cafecoton.fr | cameo.mfa.org

canvasetc.com | canwiltextiles.wordpress.com | carhartt.com | cariloha.com | caringfortextiles.com | cashmere-yarn.com

cashmere.org | catwalkyourself.com | centexbel.be | chaoticfibres.com | chicagocanvas.com | childrensformalattire.com

citrus-rain.com | clan.com | cliverichard.com | clothingindustry.blogspot.com | coats.com | cocoandcoir.com

coirboard.gov.in | colourlock.com | constantiacurtains.co.za | contrado.co.uk | cottonfarming.com | cottoninc.com

cottonworks.com | cpslippers.com | craftyarncouncil.com | creativemechanisms.com | crscrafts.com | danti.it

dappered.com | designersguild.com | designnewhouse.com | dinole.com | direct-fabrics.co.uk

diutestudents.blogspot.com | dmarge.com | domesticanimalbreeds.com | drapes-consulting.com | dressmann.com

dummies.com | duralee.com | dyeingworld1.blogspot.com | ecoursesonline.iasri.res.in | edana.org | ellisbridals.co.uk

emmaonesock.com | en.texsite.info | essentialbaby.com.au | ettitude.com | euroflax.com | fabric-house.eu | fabric.com

fabricdictionary.com | fabricforcosplayers.com | fabricgenie.com | fabriclink.com | fabricmartfabrics.com

fabricsinternational.wikifoundry.com | fabricuk.com | fao.org | farmhousefabrics.wordpress.com

fashion-history.lovetoknow.com | fashion2apparel.blogspot.com | fashionbeans.com | fashionhance.com

fauxfurinstitute.com | fdinonwovens.com | fiber-line.com | fiber2fashion.com | fiberartsy.com | fibernfibre.com

fibersoftheworld.com | fibre2fashion.com | filetlace.net | filippa-k.com | fsketcher.com | fulgar.com | garmentcare.info

garmentprinting.co.uk | garmentspedia.blogspot.com | garrettleather.com | gasketsinc.com | gauzefabricstore.com

gearsignal.com | gentlemansgazette.com | gentlemenscorner.co | goneoutdoors.com | goodonyou.eco | gourock.com

gq.com | graceeleyae.com | graciousstyle.com | hainsworth.co.uk | haydensanimalfacts.com | hespokestyle.com

homequicks.com | homesteady.com | horsehairfabrics.com | howards.fr | hunker.com | iamalpham.com | ica-bremen.org

ideaflows.net | imaginegnats.com | indiamart.com | indianmirror.com | info.fabrics.net | insidebedroom.com

instyle.com | intertek.com.hk | interweave.com | investopedia.com | iso.org | itma.com

janeaustensworld.wordpress.com | jbmartin.com | jcfa.gr.jp | jgshoe.com | joann.com | joelandsonfabrics.com

josephinesdrygoods.com | josephturner.co.uk | journal.urbanara.co.uk | jrbsilks.com | judithm.com | kalibo.org

kamakurashirts.net | kingandallen.co.uk | kirmeniplik.com | kirrinfinch.com | knitbeat.wordpress.com | knittingmagic.biz

laceguild.org | landsdownunder.com | learnaboutwool.com | leathercult.com | leatherhoney.com | leatherworldtech.com

lenzing.com | lesouk.co | lifeafterdenim.com | lilysilk.com | llamacanada.com | luckyandme.com | lunaticfringeyarns.com

lushescurtains.com | lyocell.info | madehow.com | maggiesottero.com | medeponyms.blogspot.com

merriam-webster.com | miafratino.com | miamileather.ca | midweststitch.com | miele.co.nz | mitchellfauxleathers.com

mmra.pt | modexlusive.com | mohairbearmakingsupplies.co.uk | montanatrappers.org | moodfabrics.com mordorintelligence.com | mountainsforeverybody.com | mrtx.co.jp | mrvacandmrssew.com | museumtextiles.com

muskoxfarm.org | mybluprint.com | mytextilenotes.blogspot.com | naturalclothing.com | naturalcoirindustries.com

nca-i.com | newcreationinc.com | nonwovenexperts.com | norwaygeographical.com | nptel.ac.in | nunavutqiviut.com

nvevolutia.com | nwyarns.com | nyfashioncenterfabrics.com | octaneseating.com | oecotextiles.wordpress.com

oldbullshorts.com | oldedogsewing.com | oliverands.com | olorun-sports.com | onecashmere.com | onlinefabricstore.net

organiccotton.org | oureverydaylife.com | overstock.com | owmnahar.com | paradisefibers.com | parkinfabrics.co.uk

pdfs.semanticscholar.org | peacockalley.com | perfectlybasics.com | peroni.com | peta.org | petitecoco.ro

petpostindustrialflakesbyfiberpartner.wordpress.com | pettyjohnscleaning.com | philippeperzi.com | pimacott.com

pinecrestfabrics.com | plasticsinsight.com | plastiquarian.com | plisowanie.com.pl | polyesterspunyarns.com

polymerdatabase.com | prestige-impex.com | pronovias.com | propercloth.com | pubs.sciepub.com

pushkarsingh666.wordpress.com | qiveut.com | qtag.com | quiltingdigest.com | renaissancefabrics.net | rexfabrics.com

ronanfibers.com | sacredvalleyexpats.com | sailsandcanvas.co.uk | samanthagracedesigns.com

samatoa.lotus-flower-fabric.com | sandwichfashion.nl | sarafinafiberart.com | scp.co.uk | seamwork.com | seneca.co.nz

senestudio.com | sewcratic.com | sewcurvy.com | sewguide.com | sewmeyourstuff.wordpress.com

sewobsessed.offsetwarehouse.com | shannonfabrics.com | sheepandstitch.com | shirtspace.com | shop.mybluprint.com

shop.newtess.com | shopwellwithyou.org | silicones.elkem.com | silkbaron.com | simple-knitting.com

simplififabric.com | sinsengguan.com | sioencoating.com | sisal.ws | sourcenonwoven.com | spechlervogel.com

springfieldleather.com | sprucelane.com | starcommva.com | startupfashion.com | statementsstore.com | stitchfix.com

stitchingmall.com | stmichaelsfashions.com | style2designer.com | suitstyles.com | sustainablefashion.com.au

swicofil.com | szbestbags.com | tableskirtingclip.com | tanatexchemicals.com | tandyleather.com

technicalnonwovens.com | technicaltextile.net | technicaltextile.net | teijinaramid.com | textileapex.blogspot.com

textilechapter.blogspot.com | textilecourse.blogspot.com | textilefashionstudy.com | textilefocus.com

textileglossary.com | textileguide.chemsec.org | textilehelpguide.blogspot.com | textilelearner.blogspot.com

textilelive.com | textilemates.com | textilemerchandising.com | textileresourcecenter.org | textileschool.com

textilesofindia.in | textilestudent.com | textilestudycenter.com | textiletoday.com.bd | textiletutors.blogspot.com

the-sewing-partner.com | theawardshop.com | thecottonlondon.com | thedreamstress.com | thefabricofourlives.com

thefreedictionary.com | thefutonshop.com | thelaundress.com | themohairstore.co.nz | thepolohouse.blogspot.com

thespruce.com | thesprucecrafts.com | thetrendychickblog.com | threadsmagazine.com | tianello.com | tikp.co.uk

tissura.com | tohproblemkyahai.com | townandcountrymag.com | trc-leiden.nl | trustedclothes.com | tyndaleusa.com

ukfabricsonline.com | uksailmakers.com | ullushop.com | ultimatebridesmaid.com | ultra-fresh.com | undershirts.co.uk

uomtextiletech.blogspot.com | utsavpedia.com | vacord.com | velufur.com | verolinens.com | vintagefashionguild.org

voguefabricsstore.com | vogueknitting.com | vsf-inc.com | walterychina.com | wedding.allwomenstalk.com

weddinggownpreservationkit.com | wetlaid-nonwoven.com | whatispolyester.com | whatisviscose.com

wigglesworthfibres.com | wildfibres.co.uk | windyvalleymuskox.net | woolmark.com | xacus.com |

yarwoodleather.com | zsfabrics.com

BOOK REFERENCES

A History of Handmade lace, F. Nevill Jackson & E. Jesurum, Obscure Press

All about Fabrics: An Introduction to Needlecraft, Stephanie K. Holland, Oxford University Press

Biomass and Bioenergy, Hakeem K., Jawaid M. & Rashid U., Springer, Cham

Claire Shaeffer's fabric sewing guide (2nd Edition), Claire B Shaeffer, Krause Publications

Clothing Technology (2nd Edition), Hannelore Eberle, Verlag Europa-Lehrmittel Nourn

Contemporary Knitwear Handbook: from fibre to finished garment, Arkin Ng

Fabrics A to Z, Dana Willard, Stewart, Tabori and Chang

Fabric reference (4th Edition), Mary Humphries, Pearson

Fashionpedia, Fashionary International Ltd.

Fashion Fibers: Designing For Sustainability, Annie Gullingsrud, Fairchild Books

Fabric for fashion: The swatch book (2nd Edition), Clive Hallett and Amanda Johnston, Laurence King Publishing Ltd

Focus on Fabrics, Dorothy Siegert Lyle, National Institute of Drycleaning

From fiber to fabric: The essential Guide to Quiltmaking Textiles, Harriet Hargrave, C&T Publishing

Handbook of Textile Fibre Structure: Volume 1: Fundamentals and Manufactured Polymer Fibres, Stephen Eichhorn, J. W. S. Hearle, M Jaffe &T Kikutani, Woodhead Publishing

Handbook of Textile Fibres: Man-Made Fibres, J. Gordon Cook, Woodhead Publishing

Interior textiles: Fabrics, Application, and Historic Style, Karla J. Nielson, John Wiley & Sons, Inc.

J.J. Pizzuto's Fabric science (10th Edition), Allen C Cohen Ingrid Johnson, Fairchild Books

Pocket fibers expert: a practical handbook on textile fibers : includes basic & advanced information, Irfan Ahmed Shaikh, Textile Info Society

Process Control in Textile Manufacturing, Abhijit Majumdar, Apurba Das, R Alagirusamy, V K Kothari, Woodhead Publishing

Taste and Fashion - From the French Revolution to the Present Day, James Laver, Naismith Press

Textiles (12th Edition), Sara J. Kadolph Sara B. Marcketti, Pearson

Textiles: concepts and principles (3rd Edition), Virginia Hencken Elsasser, Fairchild Books

Textile and Clothing Design Technology, Tom Cassidy, Goswami, CRC Press

Textile handbook, Hong Kong Cotton Spinners Association. Hong Kong Productivity Council, Hong Kong : Hong Kong Cotton Spinners Association

The Anstey Weston guide to textile terms, H Anstey (Helen) T Weston, Weston Publishing Ltd

The Chemical Technology of Textile Fibres - Their Origin, Structure, Preparation, Washing, Bleaching, Dyeing, Printing and Dressing, Georg Von Georgievics, Read books Ltd.

The fashion designer's textile directory: the creative use of fabrics in design (2nd Edition), Gail Baugh, Barron's Educational Series

The mood guide to fabric and fashion, Mood designer fabrics, Stewart, Tabori and Chang

The yarn book: how to understand, design, and use yarn, Penny Walsh, A. & C. Black

Understanding fabrics: from fiber to finished cloth, Debbie Ann Gioello, Fairchild Books

服地の基本がわかるテキスタイル事典, 間間正雄 監修, ナツメ社

JOURNAL REFERENCES

Fiber from Milk Byproducts - A New Dimension, Neha C., Nisha A., Suman S., International Journal of Current Microbiology and Applied Science, Vol 7, issue 4

Functional finishes for textiles: Improving comfort, Performance and Protection, Paul, R.

Fibers from Casein, Innovative Biofibers from Renewable Resources, Reddy N., Yang Y.

Kapok in technical textiles, Rijavec, Tatjana., Tekstilec 51, 10v-12

Structure and properties of coir fibres, Satyanarayana K.G., Kulkarni A.G. & Rohatgi P.K., Proc. Indian Acad Sci, Vol 4

UV Protective Finishes for Textiles, Singh N., Pant S., Gill P., Parmar M.S., International Dyer, Vol 199, Issue 1

Soybean protein fibers (SPF), Tatjana R., Recent Trends for Enhancing the Diversity and Quality of Soybean Produces, Vol. 10

FABRICS

calicolaine.co.uk | fabrics.com | fabricwholesaledirect.com | libertylondon.com | moodfabrics.com
onlinefabricstore.net | S.Nine by Susanna Soo | Suit Artisan | Fordrich (HK) Limited | Knit Sources | Swatch On
Right Link Knitwear Ltd | Kokui | John (hat)

FIBERS

wildfibres.co.uk | Wuxi Maoyuanji Import And Export Co., Ltd | Bemberg